ARE MY BABIES IN HEAVEN?

A GRIEVING PASTOR FINDS COMFORT IN THE GOD OF SCRIPTURE

NATHAN W. TUCKER

1689
Reformed Baptist Press

Copyright © 2025 Nathan W. Tucker
All rights reserved.

All Scripture quotations, unless otherwise indicated, are taken from the New King James Version (NKJV), copyright (c) 1982 by Thomas Nelson, Inc. Used by permission. All rights reserved.

Scripture quotations marked NYLT are taken from *The Holy Bible*, New Young's Literal Translation (NYLT), copyright (c) 2024 by Nathan W. Tucker. The NYLT is the author's own modernization of Young's Literal Translation (YLT).

Scripture quotations marked ESV are taken from *The Holy Bible*, English Standard Version (ESV), copyright (c) 2016 by Crossway, a publishing ministry of Good News Publishers. Used by permission. All rights reserved.

Scripture quotations marked NIV84 are taken from The Holy Bible, New International Version (c) 1973, 1984 by International Bible Society. Used by permission of Zondervan Publishing House. All rights reserved.

Scripture quotations marked CSB are taken from The Holy Bible, Christian Standard Bible (c) 2017 by Holman Bible Publishers. Used by permission. All rights reserved.

ISBN: 979-8-218-63366-0

1689
Reformed Baptist Press

PREVIOUS PRAISE FOR NATHAN TUCKER

"I have to say, I'm always impressed with what you write." —Craig Robinson, editor of theiowarepublican.com

"Thank you...for your spirited argument, which advances the important argument." —George F. Will

"Brilliant...excellent." Jan Mickelson, host of WHO Radio's *Mickelson in the Morning*

"I think it is very, very good." —Steve Deace, syndicated talk radio host

"Your writing is smart and interesting." —*The Philadelphia Inquirer*

"Your command of the material is impressive." —*Akron Beacon Journal*

Dedicated to all those who have suffered the heartbreaking loss of an unborn baby, infant, or child with profound intellectual disabilities. My prayer for you is that:

[14] For this reason I bow my knees to the Father of our Lord Jesus Christ, [15] from whom the whole family in heaven and earth is named, [16] that He would grant you, according to the riches of His glory, to be strengthened with might through His Spirit in the inner man, [17] that Christ may dwell in your hearts through faith; that you, being rooted and grounded in love, [18] may be able to comprehend with all the saints what is the width and length and depth and height— [19] to know the love of Christ which passes knowledge; that you may be filled with all the fullness of God. [20] Now to Him who is able to do exceedingly abundantly above all that we ask or think, according to the power that works in us, [21] to Him be glory in the church by Christ Jesus to all generations, forever and ever. Amen.
(Eph. 3:14-21)

The author wishes to express his heartfelt gratitude to all those who have taken of their valuable time to edit this material and offer suggestions to make this book better. All errors and mistakes in this book are my own. The author would be indebted to any reader who, so desiring, wishes to send corrections to him at reformedbaptistpress@gmail.com.

TABLE OF CONTENTS

	Preface	i
1	Sola Scriptura	1
2	All Life Is Sacred	25
3	United with the First Man Adam	33
4	Regeneration—United with the Second Adam Jesus Christ	49
5	What About Those Who Have Never Heard the Gospel?	55
6	Can We Sever the First Man Adam?	61
7	Examining Other Proof Texts	97
8	How, Then, Can They Be Saved?	119
9	God Alone Is Enough	124

PREFACE

This book is not intended to be autobiographical in the least. It is not about the multiple miscarriages my wife and I have suffered in trying to have children. It is not about the tears that stain these words as I write this preface on what would have been the first birthday of one of our babies whom we lost at seven weeks. We are not seeking your sympathy. Nor do our experiences give us any kind of authority on this subject.

But I do completely understand the heartache that prompts grieving parents to ask the question of whether their child is in heaven or hell. It is a question that we have asked ourselves multiple times and that has driven me to honestly search the Scriptures for the comfort that only the God who wrote them can provide. Our experiences, feelings, and ideas mean nothing; only what God says is decisive.

But as I've wrestled with this question over the past several years, I have become troubled by several dangerous implied assumptions that underlie it. These assumptions are almost always unspoken, and the questioner is often blind to them. But unless they are recognized, understood, and checked, they can lead to very treacherous theological conclusions.

The first of these dangerous implied assumptions is that we can speak unequivocally where Scripture is silent. The Bible does not explain everything. Therefore, if we find only inferences in Scripture but no concrete answers as we journey together through these tough issues, we must be willing to humbly admit that, "I don't know with certainty because the Bible doesn't say with certainty,"

The second troubling assumption implied in the question is that babies[1] and those who have profound intellectual and developmental disabilities (hereinafter "profound IDD") are innocent and deserve to go to heaven. Or, at the very least, that they do not deserve to go to hell. It portrays a very humanistic, man-centered view of human nature that undermines the original sin, total depravity, and inherited guilt with which we are imputed with from our First Man Adam. Hell is our default destination, and there is nothing innocent or mitigating about these individuals at all. We must be willing to confess that everyone, including these individuals, deserves hell but for God's electing grace.

The third and related dangerous assumption implied in the question is that babies and those with profound IDD *deserve* God's grace because of X, Y, or Z reason. That their infancy or mental disability *demands* God's clemency. This argument undermines, or at least resists and disputes, God's absolute sovereignty in election. As we study this issue, we must be willing to acknowledge that God's sovereign grace cannot be manipulated or controlled by any condition or cause in the individual himself but is owing solely to the secret counsel and good pleasure of His will.

The fourth and related dangerous assumption implied in the question is that these individuals, but not others, are more deserving of God's grace because of X, Y, or Z. In other words, the assumption is that babies and those with profound IDD are entitled to God's grace because of their incompetency but, for instance, their cousin who became severely mentally disabled at age twenty and spent the remaining eighty years of his life without the ability to

---

[1] The term *babies* is used inclusive of all children dying in infancy, whether born or unborn.

repent and believe the Gospel doesn't. Or their grandmother who lived the last ten years of her life in a comma doesn't. Or their firefighter father who, due to injuries sustained in the line of duty, lived the last five days of his life unconscious on life support. We must be willing to repent of such an argument as specious, repugnant, and arrogant to assume that we can stand in the place of God and decide who deserves this or that.

The fifth and final troubling implied assumption in the question is that babies and those with profound IDD would have responded to the Gospel message if only they had had the opportunity to hear and understand it. It is very much akin to the question of what happens to the isolated tribesman who has never heard the name of Christ. Such an argument oozes of humanistic, man-centeredness, forgetting that owing to total depravity no one has the ability, left to their own power, to respond to the Gospel in penitent faith. God must first give the ability to come to Him in the process of the New Birth. As we labor through these complicated issues, we must confess that no one—baby, those with profound IDD, or mature, responsible adult—is capable of saving himself but it is owing solely to God's sovereign grace.

I conclude this preface with one final caution. It isn't necessarily an implied assumption, but rather a natural tendency on the part of those whose hearts have been assured that their babies will be in heaven. They tend to look forward to heaven to see their children just as much, if not more, as they do to see Christ. But as Augustine warns us, "He loves Thee too little, who loves anything together with Thee, which he loves not for Thy sake." In other words, if we aren't loving heaven and all its blessings, including reunion with family members, for

Christ's sake, we aren't really loving Christ. Rather, we are simply blasphemously using Him to get what we want.

As we investigate the hope that the God of the Bible gives to grieving and heartbroken parents, let us be mindful to avoid these dangerous assumptions and cautions. As you read this book, it is my hope that, "Now may the God of hope fill you with all joy and peace in believing, that you may abound in hope by the power of the Holy Spirit" (Rom. 15:13).

>Nathan W. Tucker
>Omaha Indian Reservation
>Feb. 19, 2025

Are My Babies in Heaven?

LIFE IS BUT A WEAVING/THE WEAVER[2]
(By Grant Colifax Tullar or Benjamin Malachi Franklin)

> My life is but a weaving
> Between my God and me.
> I cannot choose the colors
> He weaveth steadily.
>
> Oft' times He weaveth sorrow;
> And I in foolish pride
> Forget He sees the upper
> And I the underside.
>
> Not 'til the loom is silent
> And the shuttles cease to fly
> Will God unroll the canvas
> And reveal the reason why.
>
> The dark threads are as needful
> In the weaver's skillful hand
> As the threads of gold and silver
> In the pattern He has planned
>
> He knows, He loves, He cares;
> Nothing this truth can dim.
> He gives the very best to those
> Who leave the choice to Him.

---

[2] Also known as *Tapestry*, which was often quoted by Corrie ten Boom.

Nathan W. Tucker

1 SOLA SCRIPTURA

Our search for answers to this difficult question begins and ends with Scripture. The State of Missouri is known as the *Show Me State*, and that should be the attitude of every single believer when listening to another Christian —"Show me from Scripture where you are getting your ideas." It isn't enough that the person is their pastor. Or has a doctorate degree. Or is fluent in the original languages in which Scripture was written. All that matters is what God has said. And if He hasn't said it, it doesn't matter what man says.

Scripture alone is the inspired, infallible, inerrant, immutable, sufficient, and final and complete rule on all things concerning faith and practice:[1]

1. Inspiration.

The first and most fundamental component of *Sola Scriptura* is the inspiration of Scripture. All Scripture is divinely inspired, or breathed-out, by God. We see this unequivocally established in 2 Timothy, chapter 3, beginning with verse 16:

> [16] All Scripture is given by inspiration of God, and is profitable for doctrine, for reproof, for correction, for instruction in righteousness, [17] that the man of God may be complete, thoroughly equipped for every good work.
>
> (2 Tim. 3:16-17)

---

[1] Much of this chapter, except for the third and fourth concluding implications, is taken from Chapter 1 of my book *The Five Solas: An Expository Exhortation* (2024).

The first thing to note about verse 16 is the word *all*. It is the Greek word *pas*, which means all, every, the whole, every kind of. The second thing to note about verse 16 is that the Greek word translated as *Scripture* is *graphe*, which generically may simply mean *writing*. However, *graphe* is used 51 times in the New Testament, and every single time it is always, without fail, referring to Holy Scriptures. And the third and final thing to note from verse 16 is that the Greek word translated as *inspired* is *theopneustos*. The first part of *theopneustos* is *Theo*, which means God. The second part of *theopneustos* comes from the Greek word *pneo*, which means to blow or exhale. Put the two halves of the word together and *theopneuestos* literally means "breathed out by God."

In verse 16, therefore, the Apostle Paul is telling us that all Scripture is God-exhaled. Every single jot and tittle (Matt. 5:18) of the Bible has God as its author. This is what is meant by the phrase *the plenary and verbal inspiration of the Bible*. *Plenary* refers to all 66 books of the Old and New Testaments as being God-exhaled, whereas *verbal* means that every single word, as well as its verb tense and sentence placement in the original language, was divinely inspired. The entirety of Scripture —including all of its words and even its very grammar and syntax—where breathed out by God Himself.

By *inspiration*, therefore, we do not mean that God inspired men to write the Bible in the same way that we may describe a composer or artist as being inspired craftsmen. Rather, by the term *inspiration* we mean that it is God Himself speaking through human actors. However, this, in turn, does not mean that the human authors of Scripture were so completely controlled by God when they wrote the Biblical text so as to erase all differences in personality and character. *God-exhaled* simply means that God superintended the work of human authors. They were not mechanical mystics whose quills channeled the Holy Spirit as they flew across the page. Neither were they merely acting as secretaries taking down dictation from God as they wrote the Holy Scriptures. All of Scripture and everything contained in Scripture are the very words of God Himself, but superintended through the agency of human actors in a mysterious way that we cannot explain but only see ample proof of on every page of the Bible.

We read in 2 Peter, chapter 1, beginning with verse 19:

> [19] And so we have the prophetic word confirmed, which you do well to heed as a light that shines in a dark place, until the day dawns and the morning star rises in your hearts; [20] knowing this first, that no prophecy of Scripture is of any private interpretation, [21] for prophecy never came by the will of man, but holy men of God spoke as they were moved by the Holy Spirit.
> (2 Pet. 1:19-21)

The Greek word for *interpretation* in verse 20 is *epilusis*, which literally means *unloosing* or *to release*. A form of the word, *epilyo*, is used throughout the New Testament to mean *unraveling*, *unpacking*, *expounding*, or *solving*. In other words, reading it in context of both verses 20 and 21, *epilusis* means that the authors of Scripture were not making it up out of their own imaginations, but rather as they were "moved by the Holy Spirit." The Greek word translated in verse 21 as *moved* is *phero*, which literally means *carried* or *borne*, which further confirms the mode of divine inspiration that we just discussed—namely, that the human authors of Scripture were carried (NIV84, ESV,

ISV, NET) or borne (YLT) by the Holy Spirit as they wrote rather than dictated to as robotic machines.

Let's look at a few other places in Scripture where it authenticates itself to be the very word of God. The book of Hebrews begins by declaring:

> [1] God, who at various times and in various ways spoke in time past to the fathers by the prophets, [2] has in these last days spoken to us by His Son, whom He has appointed heir of all things, through whom also He made the world.
> (Heb. 1:1-2)

God spoke. God has not left Himself without a witness, but has sovereignly and graciously revealed Himself and HIs will to us in a book. He has not hidden Himself from us or left us guessing as to how we might please Him. No, He spoke through the Old Testament in which He gave promise after promise and prophecy after prophecy of what He was about to do, and then He spoke to us through the New Testament in which He confirms and fulfills the Old. In the Old testament God spoke through prophets; in the New He speaks through God the Son Jesus Christ and those whom the Son deputized (Jn. 14:25-26, 16:12) to complete the cannon of Scripture.

For instance, in John 6:63, Jesus refers to His words as spirit and life, and a few verses later (vs. 68) Peter and the other apostles refuse to leave Him because, "You have the words of eternal life." We find in John, chapter 17, Jesus' praying His High Priestly Prayer the night before His death:

> [6] "I have manifested Your name to the men whom You have given Me out of the world. They were Yours, You gave them to Me, and *they have kept*

Your word. ⁷ Now they have known that all things which You have given Me are from You. ⁸ *For I have given to them the words which You have given Me*; and they have received them, and have known surely that I came forth from You; and they have believed that You sent Me...

¹³ But now I come to You, and these things I speak in the world, that they may have My joy fulfilled in themselves. ¹⁴ *I have given them Your word*; and the world has hated them because they are not of the world, just as I am not of the world. ¹⁵ I do not pray that You should take them out of the world, but that You should keep them from the evil one. ¹⁶ They are not of the world, just as I am not of the world. ¹⁷ Sanctify them by Your truth. Your word is truth."

(Jn. 17:6-8, 13-17; emphasis added)

There are many, many things that could be said about this passage, but here we will focus on the following:

- **Verse 6:** "'...they have kept Your word.'"
- **Verse 8:** "'For I have given to them the words which You have given Me.'"
- **Verse 13:** "'...these things I speak in the world, that they may have My joy fulfilled in themselves."
- **Verse 14:** "I have given them Your word..."

In sum, therefore, we see that God spoke through the prophets in the Old Testament and through His Son in the New Testament.

Space will permit us to only reference a few other verses that authenticate the entirety of Scripture as God-exhaled. In Matthew 4:4, Jesus refers to it as the very words that proceed from the mouth of God. In Romans 3:2, the Apostle Paul refers to Scripture as the oracles of God. And in numerous places the New Testament authors refer to all of Holy Writ as the "Word of God."

In fact, in over 3,800 times in the Old Testament we find the words, "Thus says Yahweh," "The word of Yahweh came," or "God said." For instance, Isaiah begins his book with these words:

> 2 Hear, O heavens, and give ear, O earth!
> For Yahweh has spoken...
> 11 ...Says Yahweh...
> 18 ...Says Yahweh...
> 20 ...For the mouth of Yahweh has spoken...
> 24 Therefore—the affirmation of Adonai—
> Yahweh of Heaven's Armies, the Mighty One of Israel...
> (Is. 1:2, 11, 18, 20, 24 NYLT)

Similarly, Jeremiah the prophet begins his book with these words: "unto whom the word of Yahweh has been" (Jer. 1:2 NYLT). And the author of 2 Chronicles states that Jeremiah was, "speaking from the mouth of Yahweh" (2 Chron. 36:12 NYLT; see also Ezra 1:1). In Exodus, God told Moses that, "I will be your mouth and teach you what you shall say" (4:12). In Galatians, the Apostle Paul writes:

> 11 But I make known to you, brethren, that the gospel which was preached by me is not according to man. 12 For I neither received it from man, nor was I taught it, but it came through the revelation of Jesus Christ.
> (Gal. 1:11-12; see also Acts 26:16; 1 Cor. 11:23)

In 1 Timothy, Paul quotes two other verses (Deut. 25:4 & Luke 10:7) and calls them both—one from the Old Testament and one from the New—as "Scripture" (5:18). In 2 Peter, the Apostle Peter calls Paul's epistles "Scripture" (3:15-16). Jude 17-18 quotes Peter (2 Peter 3:2) as Scripture. Finally, over and over again in Revelation, chapters 2 and 3, the Apostle John writes, "the Spirit says to the churches."

In short, Scripture is replete with self-authenticating statements that it is the very word of God. The entirety of Scripture—including all of its words and even its very grammar and syntax—where breathed out by God Himself. When the Bible speaks, God speaks. Therefore, to reject any part of Scripture is to reject God Himself, because it is His word.

2. Infallible.

The second component of *Sola Scriptura* is the infallibility of Scripture. *Infallibility* means that it is impossible for the Bible to contain any error or fault in all that it teaches. Because Scripture is the very words of God, they are as perfect as God Himself is perfect. For instance, Psalm 18:30 reads, "God!—perfect is His way! The saying of Yahweh is tried, a shield is He to all those trusting in Him!" (NYLT; see also 2 Sam. 22:31). Or Psalm 12:6, which proclaims, "The sayings of Yahweh are pure sayings, like silver tried in a furnace of earth, refined sevenfold" (NYLT). Or Psalm 119:140, which declares, "Your promises is well tried, and your servant loves it" (ESV).

We read in Psalm 19, beginning with verse 7:

> [7] The law of Yahweh is perfect, refreshing the soul;
> The testimonies of Yahweh are steadfast, making wise the simple;
> [8] The precepts of Yahweh are upright, rejoicing the heart;
> The command of Yahweh is pure, enlightening the eyes;
> [9] The fear of Yahweh is clean, standing to the age;
> The judgments of Yahweh are true, they have been righteous—together.
> [10] They are more desirable than gold,
> Yea, than much fine gold;
> And sweeter also than honey, even liquid honey of the comb.
> [11] Also—Your servant is warned by them,
> In keeping them there is a great reward.
> (Ps. 19:7-11 NYLT)

Finally, Proverbs 30:5 proclaims that, "every word of God is flawless" (NIV84). Therefore, since God is perfect, all of His words must be perfect as well, and consequently it impossible for Scripture to contain any error or fault in all it teaches—no less in what it states about God's acts in creation, about the events of world history, and about its own literary origins under God, than in its witness to God's saving grace in individual lives. Or, to put it another way, if God's Word is fallible, then God must be as well, which means that He cannot, by very definition, be God after all.

3. Inerrant.

The third component of *Sola Scriptura* is the inerrancy of Scripture. Notice how these components of *Sola Scriptura* build upon each other—(1) the Bible is the very word of God; which of necessity means (2) that the Bible cannot error; which in turn now (3) must mean that the Bible contains no errors. That's what the word *inerrancy* means—that it has no mistakes or, to put it another way, that it does not lie. That it is absolute Truth without error or blemish.

Titus 1:2 declares that God cannot lie (see also Num. 23:19; 1 Sam. 15:29; Heb. 6:18), and in numerous other places it declares that an essential component or attribute of God is His truthfulness (Ex. 34:6; Deut. 32:4; Ps. 31:5, 57:10, 108:4; Is. 65:16; Jn. 14:6). And because God is Truth personified, Daniel 4:36 proclaims that all of His "works are truth." Not only that, but because God is Truth personified, the Bible is adamant that, as Jesus prayed in John 17:17, God's "word is truth."

Psalm 119:160 declares that, "[t]he entirety of Your word is truth" (Ps. 119:160), and in 2 Samuel 7:28 King David of Israel proclaimed, "And now, O Adonai Yahweh, You are God, and Your words are true..." (NYLT). Psalm 119:151 affirms that, "All [His] commands are true," and Hebrews 10:23 tells us that all of His promises can be trusted because "He who promised is faithful" (see also Heb. 6:13).

In short, Scripture is the inerrant Truth of God and therefore doesn't contain a single shred of error, contradiction, deceit, fraud, or delusion within its pages. The Bible is indeceivable.

4. **Immutable.**

The fourth component of *Sola Scriptura* is the immutability of Scripture. We saw first that Scripture is divinely inspired by God. Secondly, that it is infallible or incapable of error. Third, that it is inerrant or truthful, incapable of deceit. Now, fourth, we see that the Bible is immutable or incapable of changing or failing over time. Because God is and always has been perfect, He is incapable—from eternity past to eternity future—of becoming more or less perfect. He is, consequently, immutable or unchangeable. And because God is immutable and unchangeable, His word must be as well.

In 1 Peter, chapter 1, we read:

> 22 Since you have purified your souls in obeying the truth through the Spirit in sincere love of the brethren, love one another fervently with a pure heart, 23 having been born again, not of corruptible seed but incorruptible, through the word of God which lives and abides forever, 24 because
> "All flesh is as grass,
> And all the glory of man as the flower of the grass.
> The grass withers,
> And its flower falls away,
> 25 But the word of the LORD endures forever."
> Now this is the word which by the gospel was preached to you.
>
> (1 Pet. 1:22-25)

Here Peter cites the Old Testament (Isaiah 40:6-8) to prove that the Gospel is the Word of Yahweh and therefore it lives and abides forever. In John 10:35, Jesus states that the Word of God "cannot be broken." In His Sermon on the Mount in Matthew 5, Jesus tells His disciples:

> 17 "Do not think that I came to destroy the Law or the Prophets. I did not come to destroy but to fulfill. 18 For assuredly, I say to you, till heaven and

earth pass away, one jot or one tittle will by no means pass from the law till all is fulfilled.

(Matt. 5:17-18)

And, again, in Matthew 24:35 Jesus declares that, "Heaven and earth will pass away, but My words will by no means pass away." Psalm 119:89 proclaims, "To the age, O Yahweh, Your word is set up in the heavens" (NYLT), and a few verses later, in 160, "and every one of Your righteous judgments endures forever." Consequently, just as God is immutable and unchangeable, so His word is immutable and unchangeable as well.

5. **Sufficient.**

The fifth component of *Sola Scriptura* is the sufficiency of Scripture. The Bible is entirely and completely sufficient to give the knowledge of God and His will which is necessary for salvation.

In Joshua, chapter 1, we find Yahweh telling Joshua after the death of Moses:

> [7] "Only be strong and very courageous, that you may observe to do according to all the law which Moses My servant commanded you; do not turn from it to the right hand or to the left, that you may prosper wherever you go. [8] This Book of the Law shall not depart from your mouth, but you shall meditate in it day and night, that you may observe to do according to all that is written in it. For then you will make your way prosperous, and then you will have good success."
>
> (Josh. 1:7-8)

God is telling Joshua that everything he needs to know about God's will in order to please Him is contained within Holy Writ. Again, in Isaiah, chapter 8, we are told:

> [19] And when they say to you, "Seek those who are mediums and wizards, who whisper and mutter," should not a people seek their God? Should they seek the dead on behalf of the living? [20] To the law and to the testimony! If they do not speak according to this word, it is because there is no light in them.
>
> (Is. 8:19-20)

There is no need for any other revelation because everything necessary for God's glory and man's salvation is contained within Holy Writ. In Luke, chapter 16, we find Jesus telling a parable in which a rich man in hell is talking with Abraham in heaven:

> [27] "Then [the rich man] said, 'I beg you therefore, father [Abraham], that you would send [Lazarus] to my father's house, [28] for I have five brothers, that he may testify to them, lest they also come to this place of torment.' [29] Abraham said to him, 'They have Moses and the prophets; let them hear them.' [30] And he said, 'No, father Abraham; but if one goes to them from the dead, they will repent.' [31] But he said to him, 'If they do not hear Moses and the prophets, neither will they be persuaded though one rise from the dead.'"
>
> (Lk. 16:27-31)

Here Jesus is saying that there is no need for the testimony of a dead man raised to life because all that is necessary for God's glory and man's salvation is contained within Holy Writ (see also 2 Thess. 2:2). Finally, returning to 2 Timothy, chapter 3, beginning with verse 16, we read:

> [16] All Scripture is given by inspiration of God, and is profitable for doctrine, for reproof, for correction, for instruction in righteousness, [17] that the man of God may be complete, thoroughly equipped for every good work.
>
> (2 Tim. 3:16-17)

No other revelation is needed, Paul says, because Holy Writ is absolutely and entirely sufficient in and of itself for a believer to be completely and thoroughly prepared for every good work. Therefore, either expressly set down in the pages of Scripture or necessarily contained therein is the whole counsel of God concerning all things necessary for His own glory, man's salvation, faith, and life.

6. Final and complete.

The sixth and final component of *Sola Scriptura* is the finality and completeness of Scripture. Not only is the cannon of Scripture so sufficient that no new or extra-Biblical revelations are needed, but it is final and complete to the exclusion of new or extra-Biblical revelations.

In Deuteronomy, chapter 4, we find Moses commanding the Israelites:

> [1] `And now, Israel, give heed unto the statutes, and unto the judgments which I am teaching you to do, so that you live, and have gone in, and possessed the land which Yahweh God of your fathers is giving to you. [2] You do not add to the

word which I am commanding you, nor diminish from it, to keep the commands of Yahweh your God which I am commanding you.

(Deut. 4:1-2 NYLT)

In verse 1 Moses is reminding them that Scripture is sufficient for knowing God's will and pleasing Him, and in verse 2 he therefore warns them that it is complete and final and must not be added to or subtracted from. A few chapters over in Deuteronomy, chapter 12, we read:

[29] "When Yahweh your God does cut off the nations—whither you are going in to possess them—from your presence, and you have possessed them, and have dwelt in their land—[30] take heed to yourselves, lest you be snared after them, after their being destroyed out of your presence, and lest you inquire about their gods, saying, 'How do these nations serve their gods, that I may do so—even I?' [31] You do not do so to Yahweh your God; for every abomination to Yahweh which He hates they have done to their gods, for even their sons and their daughters they burn with fire to their gods. [32] The whole thing which I am commanding you—it you observe to do; you do not add unto it, nor diminish from it."

(Deut. 12:28-32 NYLT)

Here we see Moses, in essence, saying that the holy books and oral traditions of other religions are incompatible with Holy Scripture and therefore are not to be assimilated with it. Similarly, Proverbs, chapter 30, beginning with verse 5 reads:

> ⁵ Every word of God is pure;
> He is a shield to those who put their trust in Him.
> ⁶ Do not add to His words,
> Lest He rebuke you, and you be found a liar.
>
> (Prov. 30:5-6)

The Apostle Paul warns the Corinthian church in 1 Corinthians, "not to go beyond what is written" (4:6 ESV). Jude writes in the third verse of his epistle:

> ³ Beloved, while I was very diligent to write to you concerning our common salvation, I found it necessary to write to you exhorting you to contend earnestly for the faith which was once for all delivered to the saints.
>
> (Jude 3)

Let me repeat that—"the faith which was once for all delivered to the saints." Not the faith that is still being divinely inspired or revealed to the saints. But the faith that has once for all time been delivered to the saints in the Holy Scriptures. We don't have to wait for new revelations. There are no new prophets. A modern Apostle does not exist. The cannon of Scripture is once and for all closed, completed, and final. It consists of the 66 books of the Old and New Testaments and none other.

Finally, in Revelation, chapter 22, we read:

> ¹⁸ For I testify to everyone who hears the words of the prophecy of this book: If anyone adds to these things, God will add to him the plagues that are written in this book; ¹⁹ and if anyone takes away from the words of the book of this prophecy, God shall take away his part from the Book of Life, from

the holy city, and from the things which are written in this book.

(Rev. 22:18-19)

Concluding Implications:

In conclusion, therefore, we have seen that this doctrine of *Sola Scriptura* is the first and most fundamental doctrine of our theology. There are four massive implications that stem from this doctrine:

1. Supreme Authority:

First, that Holy Scriptures are the only supreme rule of faith and practice. This means that all Church creeds, councils, and declarations have a lesser, subordinate authority than the authority of the Bible. Because Scripture alone is divinely inspired by God; because it alone is infallible or incapable of error; because it alone is inerrant or truthful, incapable of deceit; because it alone is immutable or unchangeable; because it alone is sufficient; because it alone is complete and final; it must alone be the supreme and final authority, judge, and arbitrator in matters of faith.

There is no other standard that even comes close. The decrees of the popes and councils of the Roman Catholic church are man-made and therefore certainly not divinely inspired or infallible. Confessions of Faith, as beautiful and wonderful as they are in summarizing Biblical truth, are man-made and therefore is certainly not divinely inspired or infallible. The statements of this religious leader or that religious conference are man-made and therefore certainly not divinely inspired or infallible. And the words of preachers and pastors are man-made and therefore certainly not divinely inspired or infallible.

Rather, only the Bible satisfies the criteria of an objective, universal, and transcendent moral standard. Only the Bible, therefore, can bind the conscience. Only the Bible can serve as the standard by which all creeds, councils, decrees, and opinions of men, no matter how wise and learned they may be, must be tried. The Bible alone is the essence of Truth and, therefore, it is the tribunal or judge of man-made claims to the truth.

Therefore, every opinion, feeling, thought, or attitude that I or anyone else has must be governed and subjected to the Word of God. I may think that my good works will save me, but because Scripture says that salvation is by grace alone through faith alone, it is my opinion, rather than the Bible, that must change. If I think that I become an angel when I die but Scripture says no such thing, then it is my opinion, rather than the Bible, that must change. If I call good what the Bible calls evil, and evil what the Bible calls good, it is my opinion, rather than the Bible, that must change. Because the Bible is the only God-breathed, infallible, inerrant divine authority in all matters upon which it touches: it is to be believed, as God's instruction, in all that it affirms; obeyed, as God's command, in all that it requires; and embraced, as God's pledge, in all that it promises.

Furthermore, when we are told that we must obey a papal decree, or a secular law, or Native religion that conflicts with the Bible, we are to, as the Apostles did long ago, reply that "We ought to obey God rather than men" (Acts 5:29). As Martin Luther proclaimed at the Diet of Worms when he was on trial for heresy before the Emperor of the Holy Roman Empire and faced execution by being burned at the stake:

> Unless you can convince me by Scripture...unless I am so convinced that I am wrong, I am bound to my beliefs by the text of the Bible. My conscience is captive to the word of God. To go against conscience is neither right nor safe. Therefore I cannot and will not recant. Here I stand. I can do no other. God help me. Amen.

In conclusion, therefore, there is no other supreme authority for faith and conduct.

2. Exclusive Divine Revelation:

The second and related implication of *Sola Scriptura* is that the Bible is not only the supreme, but also the exclusive divine revelation of God's glory and man's salvation. Scripture alone is divinely inspired by God. Scripture alone is infallible or incapable of error. Scripture alone is inerrant or truthful, incapable of deceit. Scripture alone is immutable or unchangeable. Scripture alone is sufficient. Scripture alone is complete and final. And Scripture alone is the supreme and final authority, judge, and arbitrator in matters of faith. Therefore, only Scripture alone is God's inscripturated, special revelation; the exclusively sufficient, certain, complete, infallible, and necessary rule of all saving knowledge, faith, and obedience. It alone is the whole counsel of God concerning everything essential for His own glory and man's salvation, faith, and life.

For instance, the Apostle Paul proclaims in Romans 10:17 that, "faith [only] comes by the hearing, and hearing by the Word of God." In other words, mankind can only be saved through the exclusive message of the Bible and the

Bible alone. This is because Jesus Himself declared in John 14:6 that, "I [alone] am the way, the truth, and the life, no man comes to the Father except through Me." Or as Peter put it in Acts, chapter 4:

> Nor is there salvation in any other, for there is no other name under heaven given among men by which we must be saved.
> (Acts 4:12)

The blood and righteousness of the God-man Jesus Christ is the exclusive means of salvation, and this message is contained exclusively in the Holy Scriptures. Therefore, Holy Scripture, and Holy Scripture alone, is the supreme, exclusive, and decisive Word of God concerning God's glory and man's salvation. There is no other sacred writing or oral tradition by which a man may be saved.

In Galatians, chapter 1, we find the Apostle Paul warning the churches among the Galatians:

> [6] I marvel that you are turning away so soon from Him who called you in the grace of Christ, to a different gospel, [7] which is not another; but there are some who trouble you and want to pervert the gospel of Christ. [8] But even if we, or an angel from heaven, preach any other gospel to you than what we have preached to you, let him be accursed. [9] As we have said before, so now I say again, if anyone preaches any other gospel to you than what you have received, let him be accursed.
> (Gal. 1:6-9)

What this means is that the only true, pure, and undefiled religion is found in the Bible. Any other religion, any other gospel, any other means of salvation, is a perverted falsehood.

What this means for our message as *martus* or witnesses for Christ is that we do not equivocate on the supremacy and exclusivity of the Bible alone as the Word of God. All other so-called sacred writings, oral traditions, superstitions, and rituals and practices are false and lead to eternal death. When Christian missionaries came to my moon-worshipping ancestors in Europe centuries ago, they didn't say, "Oh, what a nice religion. Here's what we believe. Why don't we try to merge and assimilate the two?" No! They said, "Repent and believe the Bible (Mk. 1:15) or you are going to hell!"

Similarly, a missionary today to deepest darkest Africa, or the Native tribes in the jungles of South America, or the Tibetan highlands of China doesn't equivocate. He doesn't make nice. He does say, "You have your faith tradition and I have mine. That's cool, it's all relative." No! He says, "Repent and believe the Bible (Mk. 1:15) or you are going to hell!" He warns the Muslim that there is no such thing as a paradise full of 70 virgins for blowing yourself up as an Islamic terrorist. He tells the Hindu that there is no such thing as being reincarnation into a better you. He tells the Buddhist that there is no such thing as achieving nirvana. And he tells the Native American that there is no such thing as happy hunting grounds.

And his authority for doing so is not his own but rather it is derived from the Word of God. Therefore, he proclaims to them there is only one God, the God of Scripture alone. That there is only one heaven, the heaven of Scripture alone. That there is only one hell, the hell of Scripture alone. That there is only one moral code by which we are to live, and that is the moral code of Scripture alone. And that there is only one Savior and Redeemer—the Lord

Jesus Christ of Scripture and Scripture alone. And that there is only one way of salvation, and that is in Scripture and Scripture alone.

This is our emphatic and unequivocal message—that all kingdoms and nations, cultures and traditions, rituals and practices, must and will bow the knee to God and His Word in the Bible. Holy Scripture is irreconcilable with any other religion. Holy Scripture is incompatible with any other religion. Holy Scripture is intolerant of any other religion.

But the religion of the Bible is also the most loving religion in the world, for it alone will hazard everything to tell a people group—at risk of life, limb, and reputation—that they are wrong and going to hell but that the BIble offers them the only means of eternal life. The adherents of no other religion would endure, joyfully and gladly, martyrdom for such a witness, but we would.

3. Originalist Hermeneutics:

Where Scripture is silent, we must humbly and readily acknowledge that we are merely speculating. As the Apostle Paul exhorts us, we are "not to think beyond what is written" (1 Cor. 4:6). Or as Pastor Thomas Campbell once said, "Speak where the Bible speaks and be silent where the Bible is silent."

I want to illustrate this point with an analogy from law. I was an attorney for ten years with a deep passion for constitutional law. Before attending law school, I read Robert Bork's *The Tempting of America: The Political Seduction of the Law* and it changed my whole judicial philosophy.[2] As a result of reading his book, I became a Borkean originalist in constitutional interpretation, which holds that the words of the Constitution, as originally publicly understood by those who wrote and ratified it, are the law of the land and that judges, no matter how badly they wish it said something else, cannot engage in linguistic gymnastics to twist its meaning in order to advance their own political agenda.

In other words, originalism is not a guise for judicial activism, whether by conservatives or liberals. Rather, it is a philosophy of, "This far and no further." Even if he doesn't like the result, an originalist still insists on upholding the rule of law. In the conclusion to his book, Bork quotes the following passage from Robert Bolt's play *A Man For All Seasons* about Thomas More, Lord Chancellor of England in the early 16th century:

> William Roper: "So, now you give the Devil the benefit of law!"
> Sir Thomas More: "Yes! What would you do? Cut a great road through the law to get after the Devil?"
> William Roper: "Yes, I'd cut down every law in England to do that!"
> Sir Thomas More: "Oh? And when the last law was down, and the Devil turned 'round on you, where would you hide, Roper, the laws all being flat? This country is planted thick with laws, from coast to coast, Man's laws, not God's! And if you cut them down, and you're just the man to do it, do you really think you could stand upright in the winds

---

[2] I would highly recommend it to those interested in law and the courts, as well as humbly refer readers to my own book: *Constitutional Musings: An Anthology of Legal Columns*.

that would blow then? Yes, I'd give the Devil benefit of law, for my own safety's sake!"

Though More sadly resisted the Protestant Reformation, he was a man of unyielding conviction who was beheaded by King Henry VIII for opposing his divorce as unscriptural. The point of this seeming detour into law and history is that originalism applies to Holy Writ as well as the U.S. Constitution. One must not allow emotions and social agendas to determine what the text of Scripture says but rather let the text impose itself on one's heart and mind.

We cannot emphatically discern mysterious that the Bible does not reveal (Deut. 29:29). We cannot elevate to the standard of a confessional statement inferences grasped at out of desperate hope. We cannot twist Scripture to say what we want it to say, whether it is to advance a social agenda or to comfort a hurting heart.

In conclusion, therefore, as much as I would love to claim that the Bible speaks authoritatively on this issue, I'm not going to bastardize the text (and my own conscience) by speaking where Scripture is silent. Rather, I am going to humbly concede that we cannot know for sure but are only speculating based on admittedly scant evidence.

4. Promises Can Be Trusted:

Finally, because Scripture is the inspired, infallible, inerrant, immutable, sufficient, and final and completed Word of God, it can be trusted in what it says and promises. God does not promise and not fulfill His word (Num. 23:19). "Not one word of all the good promises" He has made fails, for they will all come to pass either in this life and/or the next (Josh. 21:45 ESV; see also 23:14; 1

Kings 8:56). Yahweh our God alone is God, a faithful God who keeps His "covenant of love" (Deut. 7:9 NIV84).

And it can be trusted in all that it says and promises, for all God's promises are "yes" in Christ (2 Cor. 1:20). Therefore, all of God's promises in Scripture belong to us:

> [21] Therefore let no one boast in men. For all things are yours: [22] whether Paul or Apollos or Cephas, or the world or life or death, or things present or things to come—all are yours. [23] And you are Christ's, and Christ is God's.
> (1 Cor. 3:21-23)

And if God did not spare His only begotten Son, but delivered Him up for torture and death for the redemption of all of His elect, how, then, shall He not, along with Christ, freely give us all things (Rom. 8:32)? In other words, if God already did the hardest, most difficult thing imaginable by crucifying His own Son, then certainly He will do the far easier and simpler thing for us.

Therefore, "let us hold fast the confession of our hope without wavering, for He who promised is faithful" (Heb. 10:23).

2 ALL LIFE IS SACRED

All of human life is sacred. It is precious. It has intrinsic value. Why? Because all human life is made in the image of God. We read in the Creation account that on the sixth day:

> 26 Then God said, "Let Us make man in Our image, according to Our likeness; let them have dominion over the fish of the sea, over the birds of the air, and over the cattle, over all the earth and over every creeping thing that creeps on the earth." 27 So God created man in His own image; in the image of God He created him; male and female He created them. 28 Then God blessed them, and God said to them, "Be fruitful and multiply; fill the earth and subdue it; have dominion over the fish of the sea, over the birds of the air, and over every living thing that [h]moves on the earth."
> 29 And God said, "See, I have given you every herb that yields seed which is on the face of all the earth, and every tree whose fruit yields seed; to you it shall be for food. 30 Also, to every beast of the earth, to every bird of the air, and to everything that creeps on the earth, in which there is [i]life, I have given every green herb for food"; and it was so. 31 Then God saw everything that He had made, and indeed it was very good. So the evening and the morning were the sixth day.
>
> (Gen. 1:26-31)

What does it mean to be made in the image of God? First, it means that God created us in His image as rational creatures so that we might know Him (Jn. 17:3; Rom. 1:19-21a). Secondly, it means that God created us in His image as relational creatures so that we might have a relationship with Him (Rev. 21:3, 22:4-5). To what end? Because He was needy and lonely? Blasphemy! For the Bible declares that He is the Great I Am—the uncreated, self-sufficient, self-existent, unchangeable, limitless One who has no beginning, no end, no need, and no weakness (Ex. 3:14-15; Num. 23:19; Ps. 33:11, 102:27; Mal. 3:6; Jn. 5:26; Heb. 13:8; Jas. 1:17; Rev. 1:8, 22:13).

Rather, we were created in His image to the end that we would reflect His glory! That is, after all, what images do—they are copies created to reflect the original and thereby glorify the original. As John Calvin explained, "man resembles [God] and that in him God's glory is contemplated, as in a mirror." God makes that truth abundantly clear throughout Scripture. In Isaiah, for instance, He declares that mankind, "whom I formed and made," "I created for My [own] glory" (Is. 43:7). Elsewhere the Bible states that He will be glorified in His people (Is. 44:23, 49:3). In another place the Bible proclaims that God's glory will be seen upon His people (Is. 60:2); that He will plant them and they will be called oaks of righteousness in order that He might be glorified (Is. 61:1-3). All of this was made with one purpose in mind—that "the glory of the LORD will be revealed, and all mankind together will see it" (Is. 40:5).

Third, being made in the image of God means that all human life is deserving of protection. As God told Noah after the Flood:

⁵ "Surely for your lifeblood I will demand a reckoning; from the hand of every beast I will require it, and from the hand of man. From the hand of every man's brother I will require the life of man. ⁶ Whoever sheds man's blood, by man his blood shall be shed; for in the image of God He made man."

(Gen. 9:5-6)

The unlawful, premeditated killed of another is, therefore, strictly forbidden (Ex. 20:13, 23:17; Lev. 24:17). And while capital punishment is to be imposed on such murderers, it is only to be inflicted upon the testimony of two witnesses (Deut. 17:6, 19:5; Num. 35:30) because even the life of the accused is entitled to due process.

Fourth and finally, being made in the image of God means that we are all born equal and, therefore, are all entitled equally to justice and to mercy. For, "The rich and the poor have this in common, the LORD is the Maker of them all" (Prov. 22:2). Therefore, we are commanded not to show partiality and favoritism (Jas. 2:1):

¹⁶ "Then I commanded your judges at that time, saying, 'Hear the cases between your brethren, and judge righteously between a man and his brother or the stranger who is with him. ¹⁷ You shall not show partiality in judgment; you shall hear the small as well as the great; you shall not be afraid in any man's presence, for the judgment is God's...

(Deut. 1:16-17; See also Lev. 19:15)

Instead, we are exhorted to advocate for the widow, the fatherless, the foreigner, and the poor (Deut. 27:19; Ps. 82:3-4; Prov. 31:8-9; Is. 1:17; Jas. 1:27).

Unborn Life is Sacred:

The sacredness of human life naturally extends to the unborn who are also created in the image of God. Life, after all, begins at conception. The psalmist, for instance, declares:

> [13] For You formed my inward parts;
> You covered me in my mother's womb.
> [14] I will praise You, for I am fearfully and wonderfully made;
> Marvelous are Your works,
> And that my soul knows very well.
> [15] My frame was not hidden from You,
> When I was made in secret,
> And skillfully wrought in the lowest parts of the earth.
> [16] Your eyes saw my substance, being yet unformed.
> And in Your book they all were written,
> The days fashioned for me,
> When as yet there were none of them.
> (Ps. 139:12-16)

God "forms," "covers," and "skillfully wroughts" us in our mother's womb (see also Job 31:15). He "fearfully and wonderfully makes" us while were hidden in secret in the womb. He saw us, even while we were yet unformed, in the womb and knew our future before it had even begun (see also Jer. 1:5). We find this echoed in Job's pleading with God:

> 8 'Your hands have made me and fashioned me,
> An intricate unity;
> Yet You would destroy me.
> 9 Remember, I pray, that You have made me like clay.
> And will You turn me into dust again?
> 10 Did You not pour me out like milk,
> And curdle me like cheese,
> 11 Clothe me with skin and flesh,
> And knit me together with bones and sinews?
> 12 You have granted me life and favor,
> And Your care has preserved my spirit.
> (Job 10:8-12)

God has made us and fashioned us into an intricate unity while in our mother's womb. He has clothed us with skin and flesh and knit our bones and sinews together. "As you do not know the way the spirit comes to the bones in the womb of a woman with child, so you do not know the work of God who makes everything" (Ecc. 11:5 ESV).

And just as with born humans, God skillfully creates unborn children for His glory. We see this in the story of the man born blind in the ninth chapter of the Gospel of John. Jesus' disciples ask Him about a blind man they were passing, saying, "'Rabbi, who sinned, this man or his parents, that he was born blind?'" (Jn. 9:2). Jesus' response is foundational to understanding God's Providence (i.e., the goal and means of His sovereignty), "'Neither this man nor his parents sinned, but that the works of God should be revealed in him'" (vs. 3).

God intentionally made, formed, and skillfully wrought this man while in the womb to be born blind *in order* to be glorified in healing him several decades later by Christ. And so He does with each and every child in the womb. With or without a handicap or disability, God designs all unborn children with specific skills, talents, abilities, and personality in order to be glorified by them.

Therefore, since life begins at the moment of conception for the glory of God, it is equally entitled to life and liberty, justice and mercy, as any born human being. And the Bible commands that its murder be avenged:

> 22 "If men fight, and hurt a woman with child, so that she gives birth prematurely, yet no harm follows, he shall surely be punished accordingly as the woman's husband imposes on him; and he shall pay as the judges determine. 23 But if any harm follows, then you shall give life for life, 24 eye for eye, tooth for tooth, hand for hand, foot for foot, 25 burn for burn, wound for wound, stripe for stripe.
> (Ex. 21:22-25)

Disabled Life is Sacred:

Those born with mental and/or physical handicaps are no less made in the image of God and entitled to protection as their healthier counterparts. And they are no less made by God for His glory. "So the LORD said to him, 'Who has made man's mouth? Or who makes the mute, the deaf, the seeing, or the blind? Have not I, the LORD?'" (Ex. 4:11). What a breathtaking statement of God's Providence! Disabilities are no accident. They are not a random brainfart of the universe. Rather, they are designed by

God for His sovereign purposes in order to maximize His glory. And therefore their life is no less sacred, no less precious, and no less intrinsically valuable than any other life.

Nathan W. Tucker

GOD MOVES IN MYSTERIOUS WAYS
By William Cowper

1 God moves in a mysterious way
His wonders to perform:
He plants His footsteps in the sea,
And rides upon the storm.

2 Deep in unfathomable mines
Of never-failing skill,
He treasures up His bright designs,
And works His sovereign will.

3 Ye fearful saints, fresh courage take;
The clouds ye so much dread
Are big with mercy, and shall break
In blessings on your head.

4 Judge not the Lord by feeble sense,
But trust Him for His grace;
Behind a frowning providence
He hides a smiling face.

5 His purposes will ripen fast,
Unfolding every hour:
The bud may have a bitter taste,
But sweet will be the flower.

6 Blind unbelief is sure to err,
And scan His work in vain;
God is His own Interpreter,
And He will make it plain.

3 UNITED WITH THE FIRST MAN ADAM

*B*ut while all human life is sacred because it is made in the image of God for His glory, the very First Man Adam rejected the glory of God for his own and, as a result, all his progeny fell with him. Look again at Genesis, chapter 1, where on the sixth day of creation we read:

> 26 And God says, "Let Us make man in Our image, according to Our likeness, and let them rule over the fish of the sea, and over the birds of the heavens, and over the cattle, and over all the earth, and over every creeping thing that is creeping on the earth." 27 And God creates the man in His image; in the image of God He created him, a male and a female He created them. 28 And God blesses them, and God says to them, "Be fruitful, and multiply, and fill the earth, and subdue it, and rule over the fish of the sea, and over the birds of the heavens, and over every living thing that is creeping upon the earth."
> (Gen. 1:26-28 NYLT)

We are told God had created a beautiful garden (Gen. 2:8), and that "Yahweh God takes the man [Adam] and causes him to rest in the Garden of Eden, to serve it and to keep it" (vs. 15 NYLT). God created this first man Adam to never die (vs. 17). And this first man Adam was created innocent before God without shame or guilt (Gen. 1:31, 2:25).

Then Genesis, chapter 2, tells us that God gave this first man Adam a covenant of works that consisted of but a single commandment:

> ¹⁶ And Yahweh God lays a charge on the man, saying, "Of every tree of the garden eating you eat; ¹⁷ and of the tree of knowledge of good and evil, you do not eat of it, for in the day of your eating of it—dying you die."
>
> (Gen. 2:16-17 NYLT)

But this first man Adam and his wife Eve ate the forbidden fruit after they "saw that the fruit of the tree was *good* for food, and *pleasing* to the eye, and also *desirable* for gaining wisdom" (Gen. 3:6; emphasis added). And when they did so, the Bible tells us that they inherited eternal death (Rom. 6:23) though they continued, for a time, to physically live (1 Tim. 5:6).

Mankind's problem, therefore, is that in the *very same sin* that Adam sinned, all mankind sinned as well. Romans, chapter 5, makes this explicit:

> Therefore, just as sin entered the world through one man, and death through sin, and in this way death came to all men, because *all sinned*.
>
> (Rom. 5:12 NIV84; emphasis added)

We see this confirmed in five other places throughout the fifth chapter of Romans:

- **Verse 15:** By "the one man [Adam's] offense many died."
- **Verse 16:** "[T]he judgment which came from one offense resulted in condemnation."

- **Verse 17:** "[B]y the one man [Adam's] offense death reigned through the one."
- **Verse 18:** "[T]hrough one man [Adam's] offense judgment came to all men, resulting in condemnation."
- **Verse 19:** "[B]y one man [Adam's] disobedience many were made sinners."

Let me restate these five verses in reverse order to help make it clearer:

(1) by the *very same* sin of our first parent Adam, all humanity was made—or imputed—to have committed the same sin as well (vs. 12 & 19); and therefore

(2) all men are imputed from the moment of conception to be as guilty and unrighteous as Adam and consequently under God's rightful judgment (vs. 18) and condemnation (vs. 16, 18); which

(3) resulted in both physical and spiritual death for all men (vs. 15, 17; see also 1 Cor. 15:45-49).

This has traditionally been called the doctrine of original sin, which consists of three inseparable components:

(1) Imputed sin;
(2) Imputed guilt; and
(3) Total depravity.

1. *Imputed sin* (or *original sin* or *inherited sin*) means that the First Man Adam's sin has been imputed—or conveyed, reckoned, accounted—to every single one of his progeny. When Adam disobeyed God by eating of the apple, all humanity also disobeyed by eating of the apple. Adam's sin is every bit our sin.

Our first man Adam was our federal head. Much like an agent binds the principal, a politician the constituents he represents, or an athlete the team he plays on, so Adam's actions were legally binding on his progeny. In this case of the covenant of works which God imposed on Adam, God viewed humanity as a corporate entity represented by its first parent.

To illustrate, the 2004 movie *Troy* opens with a scene in which two armies face off against each other. But rather than sending everyone into battle, the opposing kings choose a single soldier to represent them in a duel and whoever's champion won, won the entire field of battle for his liege. One side chose the giant Boagrius and the other side Achilles, and when Achilles won, the entire army he represented won in his victory as well. And when the giant Boagrius lost, his lost was imputed to every single man in the army he represented.

We see the same thing illustrated in the story of David and Goliath:

> [3] The Philistines were standing on one hill, and the Israelites were standing on another hill with a ravine between them. [4] Then a champion named Goliath, from Gath, came out from the Philistine camp. He was nine feet, nine inches tall [5] and wore a bronze helmet and bronze scale armor that weighed one hundred twenty-five pounds. [6] There was bronze armor on his shins, and a bronze javelin was slung between his shoulders. [7] His spear shaft was like a weaver's beam, and the iron point of his spear weighed fifteen pounds. In addition, a shield-bearer was walking in front of him.

⁸ He stood and shouted to the Israelite battle formations, "Why do you come out to line up in battle formation?" He asked them, "Am I not a Philistine and are you not servants of Saul? *Choose one of your men and have him come down against me. ⁹ If he wins in a fight against me and kills me, we will be your servants. But if I win against him and kill him, then you will be our servants and serve us."* ¹⁰ Then the Philistine said, "I defy the ranks of Israel today. Send me a man so we can fight each other!"

(1 Sam. 17:3-10 CSB; emphasis added)

Goliath, like the first man Adam, was defeated, and all the Philistine army, like Adam's progeny, shared in his defeat.

2. *Imputed guilt* means that the First Man Adam's guilt has been imputed—or conveyed, reckoned, accounted—to every single one of his progeny. When God passed judgment on Adam, He passed judgment on all mankind in Adam as well. Every single one of us. All of Adam's descendants. Without exception. "Death came to all men, because *all sinned*" (Rom. 5:12 NIV84; emphasis added). And consequently all men are conceived already judged and condemned in Adam (vs. 17). From the moment of conception we are already "by nature children of wrath" (Eph. 2:3) who are "condemned already" (Jn. 3:18) with "the wrath of God abid[ing] on [us]" (vs. 36).

All of us are conceived as children of hell. For we have all fallen short of the glory of God (Rom. 3:23) and, consequently, the wages of such sin is eternal death (Rom. 6:23) in hell. We read, for instance, in Luke, chapter 16, of a rich man who was in, "'torments in Hades'" (vs. 23).

Notice the plural—torments. This is not mere torment, but the worst torture imaginable, multiplied by infinity. This is confirmed in verse 24, where we find him telling Abraham, """...for I am tormented in this flame!""" He is in so much torment that even a single drop of water carried a long distance on the tip of a finger would seem like heaven to one who had only been there five seconds.

In another place Jesus tells us that hell is a furnace of fire in outer darkness where we will be wailing and gnashing our teeth (Matt. 8:12, 13:42, 50, 24:51). He warns that it is the destruction of our soul (Matt. 10:28) in a fire that shall never be quenched and where our worm does not die (Mk. 9:44, 46, 48; see also Is. 66:24). Furthermore, the book of Revelation describes hell as a place of torment with burning sulfur (14:10) in a lake of fire (20:15).

This is the default destiny of every single one of us without exception. We sinned in Adam, and therefore we share in Adam's guilt and just punishment. Just as every single man in Boagrius' army suffered the same consequences as he did in his defeat to Achilles, and just as every football player shares in their teammates fifteen-yard penalty, so we, too, are imputed with the guilt of our federal head.

3. *Total depravity* refers to the First Man Adam's corrupt sin nature (traditionally called *original pollution*) that has been imputed—or conveyed, reckoned, accounted—to every single one of his progeny. For the Bible tells us that we are not born as an innocent blank slate free to choice whether to be either good or bad. Rather, as a descendent of the First Man Adam, we have had our sin nature from the moment of our conception. For instance, the psalmist declares, "Surely I was sinful at birth, sinful from the time my mother conceived me" (Ps. 51:5 NIV84). Elsewhere we read, "Even from birth the wicked go astray; from the womb they are wayward and speak lies" (Ps. 58:3 NIV84). Therefore, the problem we have is not that we commit sins, but that we are sinful. We are not a sinner because we commit sins, we commit sins because we are a sinner.

Not merely our actions, thoughts, or behaviors, but we ourselves are sin. Our soul is black as night and uglier than hell. We have been as grotesque in our evil as any demon of hell from the moment we were conceived and, therefore, have always been under the rightful sentence of eternal damnation. This is why we sin—because we have been a sinner from conception. This is why we cannot stop sinning—because we have been a sinner from conception. This is why we will die a physical death—because we have been a sinner from conception. This is why we will roast for all eternity in hell—because we are a sinner from conception.

And we not only commit evil acts because we are inherently evil, but because we delight in our evil (Prov. 2:14, 21:10). We have a sin nature of inborn, spiteful rebellion against God that we cannot reform on our own. We cannot tame it. We cannot control it. We are hardwired to sin and cannot stop doing it. We have become its slave, for Jesus tells us that, "'Most assuredly I say to you, whoever commits sin is a slave of sin'" (Jn. 8:34). The Apostle John writes, "[8] He who sins is of the devil, for the devil has sinned from the beginning...[6] Whoever sins has neither seen God nor known Him" (1 John 3:8, 6).

The book of Genesis points out the obvious, "...the wickedness of man [i]s great in the earth, and that every intent of the thoughts of his heart [i]s only evil continually" (Gen. 6:5). It isn't for naught that a two-year-old's favorite word is, "No!" We do not have to train our children to be bad, but to be good. And as every parent knows, if we do not discipline our children, they will do whatever is right in their own selfish eyes.

Let's say that on my right hand I had a gourmet meal freshly prepared and laid out on the finest of china, and on my left hand I had pig slop. If I brought a hog into this room, which meal do you think he is going to go to? It is a hog. It doesn't care about the culinary arts or fine dining, it wants slop. He was conceived and born with a desire for filth.

And so were all of us in the First Man Adam. "Can the Ethiopian change his skin or the leopard its spots? Neither can you do good who are accustomed to doing evil" (Prov. 13:23). As God Himself proclaims, "'The heart is deceitful above all things, and desperately wicked; who can know it?'" (Jer. 17:9). The author of the book of Job writes, "What is man that he could become pure?" (Job 15:14; see also Job 25:4), for "who can make something pure out of what is impure? No one." (Job 14:4). Therefore, the Bible concludes that no one, "can say, 'I have made my heart pure; I am clean and without sin'" (Prov. 20:9). "All of us," Isaiah the prophet tells us, "have become like one who is unclean, and all our righteous acts are like menstrual rages" (Is. 64:6 NYLT).

Furthermore, because of our sin nature, we are utterly biased against, and disabled and antagonistic toward, God. For instance, the Apostle Paul tells us:

> [5] For those who are according to the flesh, *the things of the flesh they do mind*; but those who are according to the Spirit, the things of the Spirit they do mind. [6] For the mind of the flesh is death, but the mind of the Spirit is life and peace. [7] *Because*

the mind of the flesh is enmity to God—for it does not subject itself to the law of God, neither is it able. 8 And those who are in the flesh are not able to please God.

(Rom. 8:5-8 NYLT; emphasis added)

James, the half-brother of Christ, admonishes us that, "Do you not know that friendship with the world is enmity with God? Whoever therefore wants to be a friend of the world is the enemy of God" (Jas. 4:4). In Galatians, Paul writes that "the flesh lusts against the Spirit, and the Spirit against the flesh; and these are contrary to one another" (Gal. 5:17). And in Philippians he warns that, "[18] many live as enemies of the cross of Christ....[19] Their minds are set on earthly things" (Phil. 3:18-19). Finally, in Romans 5, the apostle describes the unregenerate as enemies of God (Rom. 5:10).

Without the New Birth, therefore, we are:

- Unable to please God (Rom. 8:8).
- Unable to subject ourselves to the law of God (Rom. 8:7).
- At enmity with God (Jas. 4:4).
- Contrary to God (Gal. 5:17).
- With minds set on sin (Rom. 8:5; Phil. 3:19).
- Enemies of God (Rom. 5:10; Phil. 3:18; Jas. 4:4).

Furthermore, from the moment of conception we are children of lawlessness. For we not only sinned in the first man Adam's sin, but we also commit our own sins every single second of every single day of our entire lives. The Bible tells us that, "'no one is good but One, that is, God'" (Mk. 10:18). The Apostle John warns that, "Whoever commits sin also commits lawlessness, and sin is lawlessness" (1 Jn. 3:4). The Apostle Paul writes:

> **9** ...For we have previously charged both Jews and Greeks that they are all under sin.
> **10** As it is written:
> "There is none righteous, no, not one;
> **11** There is none who understands;
> There is none who seeks after God.
> **12** They have all turned aside;
> They have together become unprofitable;
> There is none who does good, no, not one."...
> **18** "There is no fear of God before their eyes."...
> **23** ...all have sinned and fall short of the glory of God,
>
> (Rom. 3:9-12, 18, 23)

From conception each and every single one of us have rejected and ridiculed God's right to govern our lives as we blasphemously declare to Him, "Not Your will be my will be done!" We are in a state of insurrection, of rebellion, in which the Bible tells us that everyone does what is right in his own eyes (Num. 15:39; Deut. 12:8; Judges 17:6, 21:25).

CONCLUDING IMPLICATIONS:

The **first** implication is that every single son of the First Man Adam is a spawn of Satan (Jn. 8:44; 1 Jn. 3:8; 2 Tim. 2:25-26). Everyone, without exception. Babies are simply baby spawns of Satan. Those with profound IDD are simply spawns of Satan with limitations. Everyone of us is conceived with the spiritual DNA to—apart from God's sovereign restraining hand—make Adolf Hitler look like a choir boy. This is just simple genetics. We are all devils. We are all anti-Christs. One cannot fully understand how holy and righteous God is, and how precious and beautiful the precious blood of Christ is, without first understanding how sinful and wicked we are.

The **second** implication, therefore, is that it is only owing to common grace that unrepentant sinners continue to live, for all deserve physical and eternal death from the moment of conception (Rom. 3:23, 6:23). It is an act of common grace that He continues to uphold the universe every second of its existence by His Word (Neh. 9:6; Col. 1:15-17). It is an act of common grace that He has established the sun, moon, and stars in their orbits. It is an act of common grace that He set the planters, black holes, and galaxies in their places (Job 38-41; Ps. 104). It is an act of common grace that He created the valleys and commanded the oceans to come this far and no further (Ibid).

It is an act of common grace that every single day He designs the sunrise and sunset for our enjoyment (Ibid). It is an act of common grace that He paints the tapestry of the stars for us to gaze at in amazement (Ibid). It is an act of common grace that He feeds the animals (Job 38:39-41; Ps. 104:13, 21, 27-30) and determines when they take their last breath (Ps. 104:29-30; Matt. 10:29; Lk. 12:6). It is an act of common grace that He causes the sun to rise each day and sends the rain in its season (Matt. 5:45). It is an act of common grace that every single day He takes up His pen to write a new act for creation to follow (Job 38-41; Ps. 104).

And there is nothing keeping any unbeliever out of hell at any given moment but God's sovereign, arbitrary will. God can cast them into hell at any given second. His righteousness cries out for them to be destroyed forever within its eternal fires, but it is only His arbitrary mercy that stays the sword of divine justice that is even now brandished this very moment above their heads. And God has placed Himself under no obligation or promise to keep them from their appointment with hell this very moment. As Jonathan Edwards once described their dire straits in his famous sermon *Sinners in the Hands of an Angry God*:

> The God that holds you over the pit of hell, much as one holds a spider, or some loathsome insect over the fire, abhors you, and is dreadfully provoked: his wrath towards you burns like fire; he looks upon you as worthy of nothing else, but to be cast into the fire; he is of purer eyes than to bear to have you in his sight; you are ten thousand times more abominable in his eyes, than the most hateful venomous serpent is in ours.
>
> You have offended him infinitely more than ever a stubborn rebel did his prince; and yet it is nothing but his hand that holds you from falling into the fire every moment. It is to be ascribed to nothing else, that you did not go to hell the last night; that you were suffered to awake again in this world, after you closed your eyes to sleep.
>
> And there is no other reason to be given, why you have not dropped into hell since you arose in the morning, but that God's hand has held you up. There is no other reason to be given why you have not gone to hell, since you have sat [listening to me speak], provoking his pure eyes by your sinful wicked [attitude of rebellion]. Yea, there is nothing else that is to be given as a reason why you do not this very moment drop down into hell.

And so when God killed all but eight inhabitants of the earth in the Flood (Gen. 6-8), He did so because it was just. They—babies, those with profound IIDD, and mature, responsible adults—were evil, unrepentant sinners (Gen. 6:5) who got exactly what all of us deserve from the moment of our conception. There were no innocents among them. When God killed all the inhabitants of Sodom and Gomorrah (Gen. 19), He did so because it was just. They—babies, those with profound IDD, and mature, responsible adults—were evil, unrepentant sinners (Gen. 18:20, 32, 19:13) who got exactly what all of us deserve from the moment of our conception. There were no innocents among them. When God ordered the deaths of all the inhabitants of Canaan (Deut. 20:16-17), He did so because it was just. They—babies, those with profound IDD, and mature, responsible adults—were evil, unrepentant sinners (Gen. 15:16) who got exactly what all of us deserve from the moment of our conception. There were no innocents among them.

These and other examples (see, for instance, 1 Sam. 15:1-3; Ezek. 9:5-7) from Scripture demonstrate that even babies and those with profound IDD can be vessels of wrath created by God to demonstrate His power and wrath (Rom. 9:22), and that He is free to execute judgment anytime and anywhere He sees fit. As R.C. Sproul has put it:

> The second reason God commanded them all to be put to death is because they were all, every man, woman and child of them, sinners. And the wages of sin is death. In short, God did this for the same reason He does all that He does, for the good of His people, and for His own glory.

It is because we are sinners, and because God so often showers us with grace, that we lose sight of the justice of God, and the blackness of sin. When we read about the execution of the Canaanites we ought not to ask, "How could God do this?" but "Why does He not kill us all?" The shocking part of the story of the conquest of Canaan is God's love for His rebellious people, not His just wrath toward other rebels. From the moment of our conception we are all under God's just death sentence. Every moment of every day is a momentary stay of execution. When we forget this truth we show ourselves to be the sinners we are. But praise His name, Christ came into the world to save sinners. He who knew no sin became sin for us, and died a sinner's death that we might live. May we who are called by His name never lose either the amazing, or the grace, in amazing grace.[1]

The **third** and final implication is that Adam's progeny—including babies and those with profound IDD—have no place in heaven apart from Christ. The first reason for this is, as we have seen, that God's wrath burns hot against them (Jn. 3:18, 36; Eph. 2:3). The psalmist tells us that:

> [4] For You are not a God who takes pleasure in wickedness,
> Nor shall evil dwell with You.
> [5] The boastful shall not stand in Your sight;
> You hate all workers of iniquity.

---

[1] https://www.linkedin.com/pulse/ask-rc-why-did-god-command-children-israel-kill-every-sproul-jr-

⁶ You shall destroy those who speak falsehood;
The LORD abhors the bloodthirsty and deceitful man.

(Ps. 5:4-6)

God hates all workers of iniquities (vs. 5) and abhors bloodthirsty and deceitful man (vs. 6). Unrepentant sinners cannot dwell with Him (vs. 4); they cannot stand in His sight (vs. 5). "God is angry with the wicked every day" (Ps. 7:11), for "the wicked and the one who loves violence His soul hates" (Ps. 11:5). Therefore God is incapable of tolerating even one sinner in His heaven; the two cannot coexist. Secondly, the mere presence of such a sinner would defile heaven (Num. 19:20; 1 Cor. 3:17).

Third, the inhabitants of heaven, both angels and saints, would abhor such an unrepentant devil. Because the saints of heaven perfectly love God supremely and others sacrificially, they love as God loves and hate as God hates. Therefore, even such a sinner's parents, spouse, and children would fight to cast him into hell should God give them leave. And should He restrain them in His mercy, they would shun the vile miscreant all the days of his infinite sojourn in heaven. They would want nothing to do with such a hideous, vile offspring of Satan.

Which brings us to the fourth and final point—heaven would be absolute hell for such a hater of God. Why? Because God is there. Unbelievers would rather spend an eternity in hell than a millisecond in heaven so long as God is there. Nor would his glorified parents, spouse, and children be spared his animosity, for he would hate such holy saints with such vile loathing that would hourly chaff away at his soul. He would, therefore, beg God to send him to hell rather than spend one minute longer in a God-filled paradise. Every millisecond he spends there torments his soul just as surely as the flames of hell would. It would, in a sense, be merciful to send him into the lake of fire rather than to endure the presence of his Creator.

For these four reasons, therefore, it is impossible for an unrepentant sinner still united with the First Man Adam to find any refuge in the halls of heaven.

4 REGENERATION—UNITED WITH THE SECOND ADAM JESUS CHRIST

And therefore what mankind needs is nothing less than a new Adam to free us from the just penalty of eternal death that we deserve for our sins, both actual and imputed. Our salvation consists of being justified—declared righteous—before God. And this is what happens at the moment of New Birth—you are united by *faith* with the Second Adam Jesus Christ so that His victory over sin and death is imputed to you (Phil. 3:9).

For the Bible describes the first man Adam as a "type" (NKJV) or "pattern" (NIV84) of the Second Adam Jesus Christ (Rom. 5:14). We see this contrast between the first man Adam and the Second Adam Jesus Christ clearly depicted in the fifth chapter of Romans:

> [12] Because of this, even as through one man sin entered into the world, and through sin—death, and thus to all men death passed through, for that all sinned...[15] But the gracious gift is not as the offense. For if by the trespass of the one many died, much more did the grace of God, and the free gift in grace of the one Man Jesus Messiah, abound to many. [16] And the free gift is not through the one who did sin. For judgment of that one resulted in condemnation, but the gracious gift which came from many offenses resulted in a declaration of "Righteous." [17] For if by the offense of the one death reigned through the one, much more those who are receiving the abundance of grace and of the free gift of righteousness shall reign in life through the One—Jesus Messiah.

¹⁸ So, then, as through one offense condemnation came to all men, so also through one act of righteousness justification of life came to all men. ¹⁹ For as through the disobedience of the one man, many were appointed sinners, so also through the obedience of the One shall many be appointed righteous.

(Rom. 5:12, 15-19 NYLT)

Let me restate these verses in reverse order to help make it clearer:

(1) by the *very same* obedience of the Second Adam Jesus Christ, all who are found in Him are made—or imputed—to have committed the same obedience as well (vs. 19); and therefore

(2) all who are found in Christ are imputed with His righteousness (vs. 19) and consequently declared forensically justified without fear of condemnation (vs. 16, 18; see also Rom. 8:1); which

(3) results in their eternal life (vs. 15, 17; see also 1 Cor. 15:45-49).

No one can enter heaven without perfectly fulfilling the law of God. Let no one tell you otherwise—salvation is by works...but not ours but Christ's. Christ's perfect obedience in fulfilling the law of God which we could never do, and in dying on the cross as the spotless sacrificial lamb we could never be, has become the righteousness of all those who would simply put their trust in Him (Rom. 5:19, 10:4; 1 Cor. 1:30; 2 Cor. 5:21; Phil 3:9)!

You can never make yourself good enough for God, so stop trying and simply look to Jesus as the initiator and consummator of your faith (Heb. 12:2)! This is what happens after illumination—by penitent faith one receives Christ as their supreme treasure and are united with Him! Just as in the first man Adam we sinned, so in the Second Adam Jesus Christ we are by faith considered to have been obedient! Just as in the first man Adam we were imputed unrighteous, so in the Second Adam Jesus Christ we are by faith imputed to have been righteous! Just as in the first man Adam we were declared guilty, so in the Second Adam Jesus Christ we are by faith declared to have been innocent! Just as in the first man Adam we were under the just punishment of eternal hell, so in the Second Adam we are by faith under the just inheritance of eternal heaven!

By faith alone we are united with Christ (Eph. 1:4, 6-7, 13) and all that God the Father is for us in God the Son (2 Cor. 1:20). Look at how the Apostle Paul describes the fulness of this life in the Second Adam Jesus Christ:

> With Messiah I have been crucified, and live no more do I, but Messiah lives in me. And that which I now live in the flesh I live by faith in the Son of God, who agaped me and give Himself for me.
>
> (Gal. 2:20 NYLT; see also 6:14)

By faith alone, Christ's obedience is your obedience. Christ's sacrificial death is your sacrificial death! Christ's life is your life! Christ in you is your sole hope of glory (Col. 1:27)! By grace alone through faith alone in Christ Jesus alone, we are forensically justified and adopted as children of God. Because we are by faith grafted into Christ so that His righteousness now clothes us, God has "cleanse[d] you from all your impurities and from all your idols...save[d] you from all your uncleanness" (Ezek. 36:25,

29a). As the psalmist declares, "[A]s far as the east is from the west, so far has he removed our transgressions from us!" (Ps. 103:12). The famous hymn *It Is Well with My Soul* puts it so well:

> That Christ has regarded my helpless estate
> And has shed His own blood for my soul...
> My sin, oh the bliss of this glorious thought
> My sin, not in part, but the whole
> Is nailed to the cross, and I bear it no more
> Praise the Lord, praise the Lord, O my soul

Furthermore, because we are by faith grafted into Christ, God has now adopted us as His children. As the Apostle Paul tells us, "[God] predestined us to be adopted as His sons through Jesus Christ, in accordance with His pleasure and will—to the praise of His glorious grace, which He has freely given us in [Jesus Christ whom] He loves" (Eph. 1:5-6). In the eight chapter of Romans we read:

> [14] For as many as are led by the Spirit of God are the sons of God. [15] For you did not receive a spirit of slavery again for fear, but you received the Spirit of adoption by which we cry out, "Abba, Father!" [16] The Spirit Himself testifies with our spirit that we are children of God. [17] And if children, then also heirs—heirs, indeed, of God and joint-heirs of Messiah—if, indeed, we suffer together with Him, that we may also be glorified together.
>
> (Rom. 8:14-17 NYLT)

We find this again in Galatians, chapter 3:

3 ²⁶ For you are all sons of God through the faith in Messiah Jesus...**4** ⁴ But when the fulness of time did come, God sent forth His Son, born of a woman, born under the law, ⁵ that those under the law He may redeem, that we may receive the adoption of sons. ⁶ And because you are sons, God did send forth the Spirit of His Son into your hearts, crying out, "Abba, Father!" ⁷ So that you are no more a slave but a son, and if a son, also an heir of God through Messiah.

(Gal. 3:26, 4:4-7 NYLT)

Which is why the Apostle John exclaims, "How great is the love the Father has lavished on us, that we should be called children of God! And that is what we are!" (1 Jn. 3:1). Therefore, clothed with no righteousness of our own but only in Christ's blood and righteousness, "Every Christian," as Pastor Dr. C.F.W. Walther wrote, "may apply to himself the declaration of God: 'This is my beloved Son, in whom I am well pleased!'"

As heirs of God clothed with Christ (Rom. 13:14; Gal. 3:27; Eph. 4:24; Col. 3:10), your past failures do not define you. Your current temptations do not define you. Your present circumstances do not define you. Rather, when you come to God in such penitent faith, only Christ and His redeeming and purifying love now defines you! His banner over you is now love (Song of Solomon 2:4)! He now surrounds you with songs of deliverance (Ps. 32:7)! He now rejoices over you with gladness (Is. 62:4-5; Zeph. 3:17)! He now quiets you with His love (Zeph. 3:17)! He now rejoices over you with singing (Zeph. 3:17)!

This is why we find the Apostle Paul exulting in Romans, chapter 8:

³¹ What, then, shall we say unto these things? If God is for us, who is against us? ³² He who indeed His own Son did not spare, but for us all did deliver Him up, how shall He not also with Him grant all things to us? ³³ Who shall lay a charge against the elect of God? God is He that is declaring righteous. ³⁴ Who is he that is condemning? Christ is He that died, yes, rather also, was raised up; who is also on the right hand of God, who also does intercede for us. ³⁵ Who shall separate us from the love of the Messiah— tribulation, or distress, or persecution, or famine, or nakedness, or peril, or sword ³⁶ (according as it has been written , "For You sake we are put to death all the day long, we were reckoned as sheep of slaughter")? ³⁷ But in all these we more than conquer through Him who loved us. ³⁸ For I am persuaded that neither death, nor life, nor *angelic* messengers, nor principalities, nor powers, nor things present, ³⁹ nor things about to be, nor height, nor depth, nor any other created thing, shall be able to separate us from the love of God, that is in Messiah Jesus our Lord.

(Rom. 8:31-39 NYLT)

In Christ by faith, you are clothed with His righteousness, engulfed by God's love, and that can never be shaken, altered, or destroyed in any way!

5 WHAT ABOUT THOSE WHO HAVE NEVER HEARD THE GOSPEL?

But what about those who die without ever hearing the name of Christ?[1] The Bible is emphatically clear that apart from personal penitent faith in the Jewish Messiah Jesus Christ there is no salvation. For God declares that, "Nor is there salvation in any other, for there is no other name under heaven given among men by which we must be saved" (Acts 4:12). As Jesus Himself declared, "'I [alone] am the [only] way, the [only] truth, and the [only] life. [Absolutely] [n]o one comes to [God] the Father except through Me'" (Jn. 14:6). The Bible describes Jesus as the one, only, and final sacrifice for sins, of which no other can either be offered to or accepted by God (Heb. 7:27; see also Rom. 6:10; 1 Pet. 3:18).

Elsewhere the Scriptures make clear that apart from this personal faith—received from hearing—in the God-man Jesus Christ, there is no salvation:

> [13] For "whoever calls on the name of the Lord shall be saved."
> [14] How then shall they call on Him in whom they have not believed? And how shall they believe in Him of whom they have not heard? And how shall they hear without a preacher? [15] And how shall they preach unless they are sent? As it is written:
> "How beautiful are the feet of those who preach
>   the gospel of peace,
>   Who bring glad tidings of good things!"...

---

[1] For a fuller treatment of the exclusivity of Christ, please refer to chapter 7 of my book: *The Five Solas: An Expository Exhortation*.

> [17] So then faith comes by hearing, and hearing by the word of God.
> (Rom. 10:13-15, 17)

Finally, in another place the Bible tells us that:

> [9] God has highly exalted Christ and given Him the name which is above every name, [10] that at the name of Jesus every knee should bow...[11] and that every tongue should confess that Jesus Christ is Lord, to the glory of God the Father.
> (Phil. 2:9-11)

Not Allah, nor Buddha, nor any other so-called "god." Rather, forgiveness of sins and peace with God is only possible through the imputation of Christ's blood and righteousness alone that comes through penitent faith that comes by hearing the Gospel (Jn. 1:12, 3:17-18, 5:24, 6:40, 47, 11:25-26; Acts 16:31; Rom. 10:13; 1 Cor. 1:21; Heb. 9:26, 28).

Before we leave this topic, however, it is essential to note that its premise is entirely man-centered narcissism dressed up as a question of fairness or equity. It puts God, rather than man, on the docket. It is a feeble attempt to annul God's judgments and condemn Him that we may be justified (Job 41:8).

The Bible responds to such pompous arrogance by commanding "Silence!", for "who are you, O man, to talk back to God?! Shall what is formed say to Him who formed it, 'Why did You make me like this?' Does not the potter have the right to make out of the same lump of clay some pottery for noble purposes and some for common use?" (Rom. 9:20). The questioner neither knows how righteous and holy God is, nor how sinful and vile he is!

For as we have already seen, the Bible declares us to be evil personified without any defense or justification before God. We are not good. We are not innocent. We have no self-righteousness. We are a moral monster who is just as grotesque in our hideous treason against God as any devil of hell. We are unlovable—nay, repulsively disgusting—in God's eyes with the rightful judgment of eternal hell hanging over our heads. We are the walking scum of a creation that will one day applaud God's justice of ridding the universe of our wickedness.

And the only thing God owes us is eternal damnation from the moment we were conceived. Just as God was under no obligation to save the demons of hell, so He is under no obligation to save us. God owes us no pity, no mercy, no charity, and the only reason we remain out of hell with a chance to repent and believe the gospel is owed solely to His divine, unfathomable, unexplainable grace.

God owes us nothing for any past good works we may have done. We are pure evil and wickedly corrupt and can have no hope of earning God's favor. Our sin against a holy and righteous God cannot be atoned for by tears, resolutions, good works, legalism, or any other effort on our part. Salvation is not of works but only of God who calls (Rom. 9:11). It is not of man who wills, nor of the man who runs, but only of God who shows mercy (Rom. 9:16; see also Jn. 1:13). God will have mercy on whom He will have mercy, and hardens whom He will harden (Rom. 9:18). We are completely hopeless and helpless before God (Eph. 2:12), Who alone decides whether and when to save us. And if He does save us, it isn't because He is making much of us, but rather it is so that we might make much of Him.

In conclusion, therefore, God doesn't have to save anyone. He would be perfectly righteous and just if He only saved 1,000 souls in all of human history. Or 100 souls. Or 10 souls. Or 1 soul. Or none at all. We have absolutely no moral claim on God for anything whatsoever.

If, for instance, Warren Buffet came to your church on Sunday and gave ten of you $10 million dollars, everyone in the media would be praising him for such extravagant generosity and benevolence. Only the most arrogant, self-righteous pompous fool would suggest that it was unfair of Mr. Buffet for not giving everyone in the room—past, present, and future—$10 million. Only the most narcissistic among you would argue that Mr. Buffet also owed you $10 million simply for also being in church.

Be stunned into silent worship, therefore, that God has graciously taken it upon Himself to save anyone by the sacrifice of Himself! For the Bible calls salvation an act of God's grace from start to finish, for we are "justified freely *by His grace* through the redemption that came by Jesus Christ" (Rom. 3:24; emphasis added). For the Bible declares that, "it is by grace you have been saved through faith—and this not of yourselves, it is a gift of God—not of works so that no one can boast" (Eph. 2:8). And in another place the Scriptures make clear:

> [27] Where then is boasting? It is excluded. On what principle? On that of observing the law? No, but on that of faith. [28] For we maintain that a man is justified by faith apart from observing the law.
> (Rom. 3:27-28; see also Gal. 2:16; 3:11)

Be astounded at such extravagant grace! At such scandalous love! For in order to magnify His name in the demonstration of His moral excellencies, the Bible declares to us that "God demonstrates His own love for us in this: While we were still sinners, Christ died for us!" (Rom. 5:8).

Elsewhere God tells us that: "[He] so loved the world that He gave His one and only Son"— who was "stricken by God, smitten by Him, and afflicted...it was the LORD's will to crush [Christ] and cause Him to suffer [in order to] make[] His life a guilt offering" (Is. 53:4, 10)—so that whosoever trusts in Him shall not perish but have eternal life!" (Jn. 3:16).

The reason why the God-man Jesus Christ is the exclusive way of salvation is because our sin is so vile, hell is so real, but God's love is so great that He did the unthinkable in crucifying His one and only Son in order to save His lost sheep!

Nathan W. Tucker

AMAZING GRACE

By John Newton

[1] Amazing grace! how sweet the sound,
That saved a wretch; like me!
I once was lost, but now am found,
Was blind, but now I see.

[2] 'Twas grace that taught my heart to fear,
And grace my fears relieved;
How precious did that grace appear
The hour I first believed!

[3] The Lord hath promised good to me,
His word my hope secures;
He will my shield and portion be
As long as life endures.

[4] When we've been there ten thousand years,
Bright shining as the sun,
We've no less days to sing God's praise
Than when we first begun.

6 CAN WE SEVER THE FIRST MAN ADAM?

We are left, therefore, with a dilemma—how is it possible for babies and those with profound IDD—imputed with Adam's original sin, guilt/judgment, and corrupted sin nature—to be saved if they lack the mental and physical ability to understand and respond to the Gospel message? In other words, is there a way to excuse their union with Adam?

Two Heretical Solutions:

There are two easy solutions to this conundrum that the Christian Church has always condemned as heretical. The first is **universalism**—the belief that everyone in all places at all times will be saved. Scripture is clear, however, that not everyone goes to heaven, for most will remain dead in their trespasses and sins at the time of their deaths and, consequently, go to hell. Jesus tells us that "many are called, but *few* are chosen" (Matt. 22:14; emphasis added). In other words, many hear the general Gospel call, but only few are chosen (elected) by God to be granted the penitent faith to savingly respond. In another place He warns us:

> [13] "Enter by the narrow gate; for wide is the gate and broad is the way that leads to destruction, *and there are many who go in by it*. [14] Because narrow is the gate and difficult is the way which leads to life, *and there are few who find it*.
> (Matt. 7:13-14; emphasis added)

The second heretical solution is **Pelagianism**—a Fifth Century heresy that denied the doctrine of original sin. Rather, Pelagius and his followers believed that man was born with a free will—as a blank white slate able to choice either good or evil. And unless and until an individual choose to sin, he was as innocent before God as Adam in the Garden of Eden before the Fall. For all the reasons given in Chapter 3 of this book, this heresy was unequivocally condemned at the Council of Carthage in 418 A.D.

Age of Accountability?:

But there are a number of well-meaning, evangelical pastors who seek to remain biblical while at the same time unravel this Gordian knot of infant salvation. While there are minute differences in their approach, these pastors and theologians postulate an age of accountability. Or, to put it in legal terms, an insanity defense. They argue that there is an age of maturity, of discernment, that differs from one person to another. But before an individual reaches this age of 4, 14, 34, or whatever it may be, they are excusable before God. And after they reach this age of discernment, they are no longer excusable before God.

For instance, Pastor John Piper has argued that:

> The point for us is that even though we human beings are under the penalty of everlasting judgment and death because of the fall of our race into sin and the sinful nature that we all have, nevertheless God only executes this judgment on those who have the natural capacity to see his

glory and understand his will, and refuse to embrace it as their treasure.[1]

Pastor John MacArthur, another representative of this theory, has also likewise theorized:

> We're talking about someone who has not reached sufficient mature understanding to comprehend convincingly the issues of law and grace and sin and salvation. This is certainly an infant in the womb. This is certainly an infant at birth. This is certainly a small child. And this is certainly a mentally impaired adult at any age....
> Infants who die, then, have never had anything written in the record because they've never committed the deeds, conscious deeds of rebellion and iniquity. God knows at what point they become accountable. Infants who die have been protected by God's providence from committing those deeds, those responsible acts of sin by which they would be condemned. And listen, there is no place in the Bible where judgment is based on any other grounds than the deeds of sin. It's true they're sinful by nature, but the account against them that condemns them is their deeds. God doesn't charge people with actual sins until they commit them.[2]

Or as Albert Mohler and Daniel Akin have hypothesized:

---

[1] https://www.desiringgod.org/articles/what-happens-to-infants-who-die

[2] https://www.gty.org/library/sermons-library/80-242/the-salvation-of-babies-who-die-part-1

What, then is our basis for claiming that all those who die in infancy are among the elect? First, the Bible teaches that we are to be judged on the basis of our deeds committed "in the body."(2) That is, we will face the judgment seat of Christ and be judged, not on the basis of original sin, but for our sins committed during our own lifetimes. Each will answer "according to what he has done," (3) and not for the sin of Adam. The imputation of Adam's sin and guilt explains our inability to respond to God without regeneration, but the Bible does not teach that we will answer for Adam's sin.[3]

Jared Mulvihill echoes this in writing for Desiring God:

Although Adam's sin is imputed to all human beings (Romans 5:12–14), this sin is not the basis of God's individual eternal punishment. Scripture teaches that God punishes sinners based on the sins they individually commit. Additionally, God punishes only for sins that people willingly desire and pursue.[4]

And as Millard Erickson argues:

We become responsible and guilty when we accept or approve of our corrupt nature. There is a time in the life of each one of us when we become

---

[3] https://albertmohler.com/2009/07/16/the-salvation-of-the-little-ones-do-infants-who-die-go-to-heaven/

[4] https://www.desiringgod.org/articles/cognitive-disability-and-eternal-destiny

aware of our own tendency toward sin. At that point we may abhor the sinful nature that has been there all the time. We would in that case repent of it and might even, if there is an awareness of the gospel, ask God for forgiveness and cleansing. . . . But if we acquiesce in that sinful nature, we are in effect saying that it is good. In placing our tacit approval upon the corruption, we are also approving or concurring in the action in the Garden of Eden so long ago. We become guilty of that sin without having to commit a sin of our own. (Christian Theology, 2:639)

Finally, Sam Storms argues that:

> [First]. In other words, those who die in infancy have an "excuse" [under Romans 1:20] in that they neither receive general revelation nor have the capacity to respond to it.
> Second, there are texts which appear to assert or imply that infants do not know good or evil and hence lack the capacity to make morally informed and thus responsible choices...
> Fourth, there is consistent testimony of Scripture that people are judged on the basis of sins voluntary and consciously committed in the body. See 2 Cor. 5:10; 1 Cor. 6:9-10; Rev. 20:11-12. In other words, eternal judgment is always based on conscious rejection of divine revelation (whether in creation, conscience, or Christ) and willful disobedience.[5]

---

[5] https://www.samstorms.org/all-articles/post/are-those-who-die-in-infancy-saved

1. Fundamental & Troubling Premises:

In summary, all maintain that every single son of the First Man Adam (not just babies and those with profound IDD) is not legally, forensically accounted—or guilty, reckoned, charged, or imputed—with any and all sin they may have committed before reaching the age of accountability—including but certainly not limited to their First Man Adam's original sin—by reason of ignorance, of blindness, of innocence.

I will delve into the various proof texts they use to support their hypothesis a little later in this chapter. But for now I want to address several fundamental and troubling premises upon which an age of accountability rests (whatever particular rationale is postulated). None of the advocates of an age of accountability, many of whom have taught me so much over the years and for whom I have the highest regard, actually propagate these underlying postulates. In fact, they all deny them. However, their theory of an age of discernment *only* works if these underlying implications are also true. And the logic underlying their claims has very dangerous implications for the Gospel.

The **first** flawed premise is that they redefine the biblical definition of sin. For instance, the Westminster Shorter Catechism Question #14 asks, "What is sin?" And it answers, citing Rom. 3:23; Gal. 3:10, 12; and 1 Jn. 3:4, that, "Sin is any want of conformity unto, or transgression of, the law of God." Notice that sin is not defined as a willful violation of God's law, but rather any and all lack of conformity to the law of God, even that done in ignorance.

But proponents of an age of accountability redefine sin—at least punishable sin (as if the Bible recognizes any other kind)—as willful disobedience, something which "people willingly desire and pursue."[6] Or as MacArthur has put it, sin only consists of "responsible acts of sin," of "conscious deeds of rebellion and iniquity."[7] The logical conclusion of their premise is that sin is only sin if it is done in conscious, deliberate, and knowing rebellion, unbelief, and rejection of God.[13] [8]

But by so redefining sin, they give those under the age of accountability (approximately twelve years of age, according to MacArthur) free license to sin with impunity because it really isn't sin. But furthermore, this definition of sin excludes from its scope any and all spontaneous, unpremeditated, impulsive, and instinctive sins committed *after* the age of discernment as well. Which means you don't have to feel guilty about the road rage you committed, or harsh word you uttered against your wife or kids, because they weren't willful but merely spontaneous sins. You don't have to worry about that lustful thought you had without thinking, the habitual worrying you do without thought, or the impulsive coveting you indulge in, because they are unpremeditated and, therefore, not really sin.

The **second** flawed premise, built upon the first, is that, until the age of accountability, humans do not actually owe

---

[6] https://www.desiringgod.org/articles/cognitive-disability-and-eternal-destiny

[7] https://www.gty.org/library/sermons-library/80-242/the-salvation-of-babies-who-die-part-1

[8] https://www.desiringgod.org/articles/what-happens-to-infants-who-die

a debt of sin to God. For instance, in his book *Safe in the Hands of God*, MacArthur writes:

> Throughout the history of the church, unbelief has been singled out as the primary damning sin. A person who doesn't believe doesn't obey. Unbelief always produces evil works. It is this record of unbelief and subsequent evil works that is revealed in the Great White Throne judgment; this record becomes the basis for eternal condemnation.
>
> Little children have no such record. They have no basis on which to believe or not believe. They are incapable of discerning right from wrong, sin from righteousness, evil from goodness. Scripture is very clear on this truth. Little children have no record of unbelief or evil works, and therefore, there is no basis for their deserving an eternity apart from God. As innocents, they are graciously and sovereignly saved by God as part of the atoning work of Christ Jesus...
>
> Little children are called innocent in Scripture for precisely this reason: They have no willful rebellion against God. They have no deeds of disbelief. While they may be conceived with a sinful nature, they have never had willful opportunity to exercise that nature with full understanding or deliberate rebellion. And therefore, they are innocent of any deeds of unbelief against a holy God...
>
> There is no place in Scripture in which a person suffers the judgment of damnation on the basis of anything other than sinful deeds, including the sinful deed of disbelief-a conscious, willful, intentional choice to disbelieve. Furthermore, God

does not charge people with sins until sins are committed.
Salvation is completely by grace, apart from works.
Damnation is completely by works, apart from grace.

The only way this argument works, however, is by separating the three component parts of original sin from each other. In other words, while not denying that everyone is born with a sin nature, these advocates maintain that Adam's sin and subsequent guilt are excusable because of innocence.

But Scripture most emphatically does not countenance a trifurcation between imputed sin, imputed guilt, and total depravity. You remove one, you must, of logical and Scriptural necessity, remove the others. We *only* sin because we are first and fundamentally already sinners. Scripture does not allow us to reverse the order. And therefore if we are by nature sinners, then we must also by nature be guilty.

And if by nature we are guilty, then by nature we are deserving of eternal death in hell, for even the teeny-tiniest sin is deserving of eternal damnation. Question 84 of the Shorter Catechism, for instance, answers that, "every sin deserveth God's wrath and curse, both in this life, and that which is to come." Every sin—intentional or otherwise.

Scripture will not allow you to divorce the various components of original sin one from the other, for as we saw in Chapter 3, Romans 5 teaches us that:

(1) by the *very same* sin of our first parent Adam, all humanity was made—or imputed—to have committed the same sin as well (vs. 12 & 19); and therefore

(2) all men are imputed from the moment of conception to be as guilty and unrighteous as Adam and consequently under God's rightful judgment (vs. 18) and condemnation (vs. 16, 18); which

(3) resulted in both physical and spiritual death for all men (vs. 15, 17; see also 1 Cor. 15:45-49).

Scripture clearly teaches that everyone is conceived having already committed sin—Adam's (vs. 12, 19)—and therefore no one enters into this world without already having a debt of sin to God. Babies and those with profound IDD have already sinned at the moment of conception because Adam's sin is their very own sin. And because imputed sin is no less real, sinful, and guilty than actual sin, all are conceived already judged and rightfully condemned for this imputed sin (vs. 15, 17; see also Jn. 3:18, 26; 1 Cor. 15:45-49; Eph. 2:3).

As Paragraph 3 of Chapter 6 of the Second London Baptist Confession of Faith (1689) puts it:

> [Adam] being the root, and by God's appointment, standing in the room and stead of all mankind, the guilt of the sin was imputed, and corrupted nature conveyed, to all their posterity descending from them by ordinary generation (Rom. 5:12-19; 1 Cor. 15:21-22, 45, 49), being now conceived in sin (Job 14:4; Ps. 51:5), and by nature children of wrath (Eph. 2:3), the servants of sin, the subjects of death (Rom. 5:12, 6:20), and all other miseries, spiritual, temporal, and eternal, unless the Lord Jesus set them free (1 Thess. 1:10; Heb. 2:14-15).

The **third** flawed premise is that ignorance is no defense for breaking the law. Proponents of an age of accountability argue that babies and those with profound IDD are not guilty of Adam's sin and guilt because they lack "the natural capacity to see [God's] glory and understand his will, and refuse to embrace it as their treasure."[9] Or as MacArthur has put it, they are innocent because they have "not reached sufficient mature understanding to comprehend convincingly the issues of law and grace and sin and salvation."[10] In other words,. "Real rejection has [yet] taken place...the love of sin [does not yet] exist[] in the heart...enmity with God is [not yet] conscious and willful."[11]

As R.A. Webb theorizes in his book *The Theology of Infant Salvation*:

> [If a deceased infant] were sent to hell on no other account than that of original sin, there would be a good reason to the divine mind for the judgment, but the child's mind would be a perfect blank as to the reason of its sufferings. Under such circumstances, it would know suffering, but it would have no understanding of the reason for its suffering. It could not tell its neighbor—it could not tell itself—why it was so awfully smitten; and consequently the whole meaning and significance of its sufferings, being to it a conscious enigma, the very essence of penalty would be absent, and

---

[9] https://www.desiringgod.org/articles/what-happens-to-infants-who-die

[10] https://www.gty.org/library/sermons-library/80-242/the-salvation-of-babies-who-die-part-1

[11] https://www.gty.org/library/articles/A264/the-age-of-accountability

justice would be disappointed of its vindication. Such an infant could feel that it was in hell, but it could not explain, to its own conscience, why it was there.

But this argument eviscerates the federal headship of Adam of any real meaning. Again, as we saw in Chapter 3, the First Man Adam is our federal head. Much like an agent binds the principal, a politician the constituents he represents, or an athlete the team he plays on, so Adam's actions were legally binding on his progeny. In this case of the covenant of works which God imposed on Adam, God viewed humanity as a corporate entity represented by its first parent.

The problem with an age of accountability, therefore, is that it completely severs Adam's federal headship on the grounds of ignorance. But one can no more claim ignorance and rejection—and thereby innocence—of Adam's sin than a principal can reject the lawful actions of his agent, a citizen the legislation made by his representatives, or a sports player the foul committed by a teammate.

For instance, no seller, claiming ignorance, can back out of a contract made by his agent in good faith and within the scope of his representation. No citizen can get out of obeying a law because he never wrote and voted for it, much less even knew of it's existence. No football team can avoid a fifteen-yard penalty because it was not only ignorant of, but would have rejected it had it known of, the foul committed by one of its players.

And likewise, no one can stand before the Judgement Seat of Christ and secede from the federal headship of

Adam because of ignorance.[12] Scripture and reason do not allow for such a defense. So with all due respect to R.A. Webb, I have no doubt that, should a baby or those with profound IDD be in hell, he will be far from clueless as to why he is being eternally punished. Rather, he would freely and fully recognize and admit his sin and guilt under Romans 5:12-19.

The **fourth** flaw of an age of discernment is the fatal underlying premise of Pelagianism. Now this is emphatically denied by advocates of an age of accountability. MacArthur, for instance, states that:

> No view of infant salvation which denies original sin and total depravity is true. Did you get that? No view of infant salvation which denies original sin and total depravity is true. Babies are not free from sin, they are sinners…. What I just said to you, in case you didn't follow it, is that all babies are depraved, fallen, guilty, corrupt sinners.[13]

But as we have already seen, they argue that babies and those with profound IDD are not guilty of the First Man Adam's sin and subsequent guilt because they lack sufficient maturity to sin knowingly. In other words, our

---

[12] No one can even secede from Adam's federal headship at the Judgment Seat claiming that he didn't agree to Adam's representation in the first place. God appointed Adam without our consent or even knowledge, and yet it was just, holy, and righteous for Him to do so. But lest you think God was unjust in doing so, can you honestly claim that you would have fared any better than Adam?

[13] https://www.gty.org/library/sermons-library/80-242/the-salvation-of-babies-who-die-part-1

union with the First Man Adam is severed. And consequently, guilt is conditional—it only accrues until the person commits a deed of rebellion after reaching the age of accountability.

But in doing so, however, they create a category of man without original sin. Scripture does not allow us to separate imputed sin and imputed guilt from total depravity. If babies and those with profound IDD have no imputed sin and accompanying guilt, it becomes logically necessary that they also have no sin nature. That they are not born sinful. For why should they be? For if they haven't participated in the First Man Adam's sin and guilt in the Garden of Eden, they why should they inherit his corrupted sin nature? They have done nothing to merit such pollution, such stain, such corruption. If Adam's sin is not their own, then they are sinless, and if they are sinless, how is it possible that they can be born sinful? That is a biblical and logical impossibility.

The **fifth** flaw of an age of discernment is that it logically cuts off believers from union with the Second Adam Jesus Christ and His imputed active and passive obedience. As we saw in Chapter 4 from Romans 5:

(1) by the *very same* obedience of the Second Adam Jesus Christ, all who are found in Him are made—or imputed—to have committed the same obedience as well (vs. 19); and therefore

(2) all who are found in Christ are imputed with His righteousness (vs. 19) and consequently declared forensically justified without fear of condemnation (vs. 16, 18; see also Rom. 8:1); which

(3) results in their eternal life (vs. 15, 17; see also 1 Cor. 15:45-49).

This is our only possible hope of salvation. But if we have no real union with the First Man Adam, then we have no real union with the Second Adam Jesus Christ. If we do not stand before God guilty in the First Man Adam, we cannot stand before God as righteous in the Second Adam Jesus Christ. If we are not condemned to hell in the First Man Adam, we cannot be saved to heaven in the Second Adam Jesus Christ. You cannot have your cake and eat it too.

The **sixth** flaw of an age of accountability, as indicative of its Pelagian origins, is that it is completely and entirely void of grace and mercy. This is, naturally, denied by proponents of this theory. MacArthur has argued, "All babies saved would be an act of grace…Salvation, then, is by grace" (Ibid.). Or as Matt Perman, speaking on behalf of John Piper and Desiring God Ministries, has put it:

> He is saving them because, although they are sinful, in his mercy he desires that compassion be exercised upon those who are sinful and yet lack the capacity to grasp the truth revealed about Him in nature and to the human heart.[14]

Again, merely issuing a blanket denial doesn't make logical necessity unnecessary. No one found not guilty by reason of insanity has ever walked out of the courtroom praising the judge (or jury) for his grace and mercy. Never. Why? Because he, like babies and those with profound IDD under the theory of an age of discernment, present a

---

[14] https://www.desiringgod.org/articles/what-happens-to-infants-who-die

legal claim of due process. They don't fall upon the mercy of the Court and ask for compassion. Rather, babies and those with profound IDD are arguing before the Judge of all the earth that they are automatically entitled to be found *not guilty* by reason of *ignorance*. That, as Piper has explicitly argued from Romans 1:20, they are *excusable* (Ibid). These are claims not for mercy or grace by the Court, but for the exercise of the rule of law. For justice. For due process. Sinless people do not need grace, only equity. Piper himself even acknowledges this when he argues that "God in his *justice*" will acquit babies and those with profound IDD (Ibid.).

Furthermore, to even label such justice as grace entirely bastardizes the meaning of grace. Grace is amazing. It is indescribable. It is unfathomable. It is scandalous. Why? Because it is bestowed on us who are just as evil as any demon of hell. Because while we were still sinners— rebels, enemies, haters of God—we are reconciled to God through the death of His Son (Rom. 5:8, 10). But if babies and those with profound IDD cannot sin, where is the amazement? If they cannot hate, where is the indescribable? If they cannot be rebels, where is the unfathomable? If they cannot be enemies, where is the scandal? If it is grace that even the heathen can muster, it is not divine grace:

> [43] "You have heard that it was said, 'You shall love your neighbor and hate your enemy.' [44] But I say to you, love your enemies, bless those who curse you, do good to those who hate you, and pray for those who spitefully use you and persecute you, [45] that you may be sons of your Father in heaven; for He makes His sun rise on the evil and on the good, and sends rain on the just and on the unjust.

[46] For if you love those who love you, what reward have you? Do not even the tax collectors do the same? [47] And if you greet your brethren only, what do you do more than others? Do not even the tax collectors do so? [48] Therefore you shall be perfect, just as your Father in heaven is perfect.

(Matt. 5:43-48)

Finally, grace is unexplainable. It is Indecipherable. It is imponderable. No one in heaven will be able to explain why they are there. Why God elected them. Why they were saved but their parent, spouse, child, friend, neighbor, or co-worker wasn't. All, that is, except for this class of individuals. Babies and those with profound IDD can pull out John MacArthur's book or an *Ask Pastor John* podcast and tell you precisely why they are in heaven. "Amazing due process, how sweet the sound that exonerated an innocent like me" doesn't quite have the same ring to it as amazing grace does.

The **seventh** and related flaw of an age of discernment is that it is therefore completely Christless. This, again, is emphatically denied. Piper, for instance, argues that, "Infants, I believe, do not yet have that capacity; and therefore, in God's inscrutable way, he brings them under the forgiving blood of his Son" (Ibid). Or as MacArthur has argued:

> If infants are saved when they die, by what means are they saved?...By what means? Well, I'll tell you the means. By the sacrificial work of Jesus

Christ because that is the only means that anybody can be saved.[15]

Again, just because you say something doesn't make it true. The problem here is that the baby or those with profound IDD have nothing to be saved from. They are not in a legal, forensic position to need a Savior. By their very own words, proponents for an age of accountability argue that individuals are not guilty of the First Man Adam's sin and subsequent guilt. So babies and those with profound IDD are not guilty before God because they are sinless because they are ignorant. Again, as we saw in flaw number five, if the First Man Adam's federal headship is severed, so the Second Adam Jesus Christ's federal headship is also severed. And so proponents of this theory postulate a class of individuals who stand not guilty before God by reason of a defense other than Christ's infinitely perfect blood and righteousness. That's heresy. Plain, simple, and unequivocal heresy that cannot be condemned too strongly.

The poor creatures would be without love in heaven, for whoever has been forgiven nothing loves nothing in return (Lk. 7:47). They would be clueless, having absolutely no appreciation for Christ's sacrificial love. They would be like the angels in heaven, standing on the sidelines trying to grasp such self-emptying love (1 Pet. 1:12). They would stand by in mute silence as the redeemed of the Lord sing a new song to the Lamb (Rev. 5:9-10). Never would they be able to sing the lyrics of *When I Survey the Wondrous Cross*, *And Can It Be?*, *How Great the Father's Love for Us*, *O the Deep, Deep Love of Jesus*, and countless other

---

[15] https://www.gty.org/library/sermons-library/80-242/the-salvation-of-babies-who-die-part-1

great hymns of the faith. They will have to write their own hymns celebrating due process of law in order to have something to sing about.

The **eight** and related flaw in the theory of the age of discernment is that it therefore denies God the glory due His name. The whole point of creation was so the Creator could redeem a people unto Himself by the sacrifice of Himself in the crucifixion of Himself (Eph. 1:6, 7, 12, 14). The whole point was not an unfallen creation filled with perfect, sinless Adams. Rather, the point was the exercise —the display—of God's mercy and grace on His elect and His wrath and justice on the nonelect (Rom. 9:22-23). But here we have an entire class of individuals who are perfect and sinless by reason of ignorance. They were justified by perfection apart from Christ and therefore they have room to boast before God. That's blasphemy.

The **ninth** and related flaw of an age of accountability is that babies and those with profound IDD not only do not need Christ, but they also do not need to be regenerated. The reason for this is simple—if they are excused from any imputed guilt, they also have no imputed sin. And if they have no imputed sin they cannot be born sinful. In other words, as we have already seen, proponents of this theory have created a class of individuals who are not totally depraved; who are not polluted with a corrupt sin nature. And if they are not totally depraved, they have nothing that needs regenerating. Remember, proponents of an age of discernment tell us that these individuals cannot sin. They cannot hate God. They cannot rebel against God. They cannot be His enemies. So what need do they have to be regenerated? That's scandalous.

The **tenth** flaw in this theory is that if babies and those with profound IDD are not guilty of Adam's sin and subsequent judgment, then why do they still die a physical death? That is the very point Paul is making in Romans 5:12 (and 1 Cor. 15:21-22, 45, 49)—that all men die a physical death in partial judgment because all men sinned in the First Man Adam. So if physical death is a partial judgment for imputed sin and guilt, but babies and those with profound IDDs, according to this hypothesis, are exempt from imputed sin and guilt, then why are they being punished by physical death for what they have not committed?

The **eleventh** flaw of an age of discernment is that it presumes upon God's absolute sovereignty in election. Paragraph 3 of Chapter 3 of the Second London Baptist Confession of Faith (1689) accurately sums up sovereign grace:

> Those of mankind that are predestinated to life, God, before the foundation of the world was laid, according to His eternal and immutable purpose, and the secret counsel and good pleasure of His will, hath chosen in Christ unto everlasting glory, out of His mere free grace and love, without any other thing in the creature as a condition or cause moving Him thereunto.

Salvation is completely and entirely unmerited, owing to nothing whatsoever in the creature himself. God chose us freely, voluntarily, and independently of any good or condition or cause whatsoever in us. But creating a class of individuals—babies and those with profound iIDD—who are automatically elect *precisely because* they are babies and those with profound IDD flies in the face of such sovereign grace. Some have tried to argue that:

> As Spurgeon pointed out, it is not that God chooses someone to salvation because they are going to die in infancy. Rather, He has ordained that only those who have been chosen for salvation will be allowed to die in infancy.[16]

But with all due respect to Matt Perman, this is not at all what Piper or MacArthur or anyone else advocating for an age of accountability is postulating. They are most certainly not, per se, arguing that all babies and those with profound IDD are elect. They are arguing that they are excusable. That they are not guilty by reason of ignorance. And because of *that*, God will not impute the First Man Adam's sin and guilt to them. And, only as a result of this excusability, they must therefore all be elect.

Otherwise, just say they are elect. Why spend so much time arguing for their ignorance and subsequent excusability if that has nothing whatsoever to do with the reason why they are elect in the first place? Why spend so much time explaining God's election of this particular class of individuals if such reasoning has nothing to whatsoever to do with God's reason for such election in the first place?

But furthermore, the argument is circular. For instance, let's say that God decreed that all red heads would be elect. One cannot avoid the fact that red headedness is the reason why by saying instead that God decreed that only the elect would be red headed. There is no way

---

[16] https://www.desiringgod.org/articles/what-happens-to-infants-who-die

around the fact that red headedness is the distinguishing factor between election and non-election.

Or, to use another analogy, during a job interview an employer learned that the interviewee was a Cincinnati Bengals fan. The interviewer loves the Bengals and therefore offers the interviewee the job. It makes no difference whether you say that the he was hired because he loved the Bengals, or because the employer decreed that only those applicants who expressed a love for the Bengals would be offered a job. No matter how one phrases it, the job offer was owing solely to something in the prospective employee that motivated the employer.

One final analogy. A nine year old comes before a judge for committing several serious felonies, but the judge decides to acquit him of all charges because of his age. It makes no difference to say that the judge choose to acquit him because he was a minor, or that upon assuming office the judge had decreed that he would only acquit those who were minors. Again, no matter who it is phrased, the defendant is owing his freedom solely to the fact that he was a minor. To a cause or condition in himself.

The **twelfth** flaw in this theory is that it completely undermines the efforts of an evangelist to remove any grounds for works and self-righteousness among his audience. The discussion with lost souls would simply denigrate into a debate over whether they willfully sin, or are "good enough" for God, or have an adequate excuse for sin. They are not made to feel utterly helpless—from conception—in the mire of guilt and sin before a holy and righteous God, but rather only encouraged to adopt some moral improvement plan as they continue to try to work their way to heaven. In other words, this theory eviscerates the general Gospel call.

The **thirteenth** and final flaw with an age of discernment is that, if babies and those with profound iIDD cannot be damned, they cannot be saved either. If the standard for accountability, and therefore damnability, is whether a person has "reached sufficient mature understanding to comprehend convincingly the issues of law and grace and sin and salvation,"[17] then it casts serious doubts upon those converted at a young age, such as myself (age four) and John Piper (age six). MacArthur postulates that most individuals become accountable around the age of twelve,[18] which certainly makes any conversion and subsequent baptism before that age dubious. And, perversely, it gives parents, pastors, and Sunday School teachers an incentive to delay adequate instruction to avoid accountability for as long as humanly possible.

2. Examining Their Proof Texts:

Advocates of an age of accountability cite dozens of verses in both the Old and New Testaments which they believe, indirectly at least, support their thesis. But in apparent acknowledgment of the weaknesses of their proof texts, Pastor Jesse Johnson has argued, "Again, if any of these verses trouble you, simply skip them, and let the

---

[17] https://www.gty.org/library/sermons-library/80-242/the-salvation-of-babies-who-die-part-1

[18] https://www.gty.org/library/articles/A264/the-age-of-accountability; see also his book *Safe in the Arms of God* where he inexplicably draws this conclusion from the story in Luke 2:41-50 where Jesus astonished the teachers of the law in the Temple at age twelve.

weight of the full list be enough to convince you."[19] In other words, "don't bother with proper exegesis, just be bedazzled and bamboozled by how many verses I list. Somewhere emanating out of all those verses is an age of accountability, I just know it." Very much like one of those hidden pictures within a picture where you have to unfocus your eyes to see it, so here they want you not to focus on any particular text but rather on their conclusion which they have painted for you.

It reminds me of the argument used by some to find new rights in the U.S. Constitution heretofore unknown to mankind. These progressive advocates cite the penumbra (Latin for *partial shadow*) of explicit constitutional rights to make up what they believe to be implicitly emanating rights as well. These brand new rights are simply lurking in the shadows of the actual explicit rights. "You can't see them," so the argument goes, "but we can. Trust us. We're the experts, after all. They're there, and they mean exactly what we tell you they mean." Needless to say, I don't accept theories built upon penumbras. Either they are in the text itself or they don't exist.

Romans 1:20: "For since the creation of the world His invisible attributes are clearly seen, being understood by the things that are made, even His eternal power and Godhead, so that they are without excuse."

This text, Piper's go-to proof text, does not postulate that there is a mythical excuse out there that one could argue before the throne of God but that these individuals just happened not to be entitled to it. Rather, the Greek word

---

[19] https://thecripplegate.com/what-happens-to-infants-who-die-the-nt-answers/

translated here as *excuse* is *anapologetos*, which literally means without (*an*) defense (*apologia*). In other words, they have no defense at law.

Excuse is a poor translation of *apologia*, for Paul is not talking in terms of a sob story begging for leniency, for forgiveness, for being let off the hook. As in, "Please forgive my bad behavior, but I was under a lot of stress. Or tired. Or sick." God doesn't excuse sin. He doesn't forgive on the basis of a mitigating circumstances. Ever.[20] Rather, especially in the context of Romans 1-3, *apologia* is in reference to a legal justification, to a grounds for exoneration before the Judgement Seat of Christ.

Anapologetos is used only twice in the New Testament: here in Romans 1:20 as Paul demonstrates that even the Gentiles who have never heard of Yahweh are sinners, and then again in Romans 2:1 as he argues that likewise even the hypocritical Jews are without defense before Yahweh. As Piper himself as noted,[21] Paul's argument culminates in Romans 2:9-11 and 3:9-23 in placing both Jew and Greek under God's judgment.

The point the Apostle Paul is making, therefore, is not that there may exist a hypothetical son of the First Man Adam out there somewhere who may have a justification before God. Rather, his point is to demonstrate to the religious but unconverted Jews that they are just as sinful and guilty before God as their obviously pagan Gentile neighbors. And therefore both are desperately in need of "the gospel of Christ, for it is the power of God to salvation

---

[20] https://www.desiringgod.org/articles/god-does-not-forgive-excuses

[21] https://www.desiringgod.org/messages/final-judgment-eternal-life-vs-wrath-and-fury

for everyone who believes, for the Jew first and also for the Greek" (Rom. 1:16).[22]

Deut. 1:39: """Moreover your little ones and your children, who you say will be victims, who today have no knowledge of good and evil, they shall go in there; to them I will give it, and they shall possess it.""""

The Hebrew word translated here *little ones* is *taph*, which refers to infants or young children. The Hebrew word translated *children* is *ben*, as in David ben Jesse (David the son of Jesse) or Yeshua ben David (Jesus the Son of David). It literally means *sons*, with no reference to age. We know, however, from the book of Numbers that this phrase "little ones and children" in Deuteronomy refers to those nineteen years of age and younger who were not included in the first census of those "able to go to war" (Num. 1:3, 26:64-65). It defies reason and experience to conceive that God, through Moses, is saying that all those under twenty have not yet reached a hypothetical age of accountability.

Rather, Moses is reminding the wandering Israelites why "their little ones and children" did not share in the punishment of their parents who refused to enter the promised land after the Twelve Spies scouted out the land —because they did not knowingly participate in the rebellion. In a sense, it is like arguing that all those too young to vote are not responsible for the decisions made by those who are old enough to vote. The "men of war" were the ones who refused to obey God, and therefore

---

[22] Piper's other favorite proof text (John 9:41) will be dealt with in the last part of this chapter.

only that "generation of the men of war was consumed from the midst of the camp" (Deut. 2:14).

This is hardly an argument for a general theory of an age of accountability, but merely an application of the principle that only: ""'The soul who sins shall die. The son shall not bear the guilt of the father, nor the father bear the guilt of the son. The righteousness of the righteous shall be upon himself, and the wickedness of the wicked shall be upon himself"'" (Eek. 18:20).

Deut. 24:16: "'Fathers shall not be put to death for their children, nor shall children be put to death for their fathers; a person shall be put to death for his own sin.'"

Pastor Johnson argues from this text that, "Babies will not be punished in hell for the sins of their parents—even of Adam."[23] However, original sin is not a doctrine that we are being punished for another's—the First Man Adam's—sin. Rather, it is a doctrine that we are being punished for our own sin in Adam. Therefore, babies and those with profound IDD have already sinned at the moment of conception because Adam's sin is their very own sin. And, consequently, because imputed sin is no less real, sinful, and guilty than actual sin, all are conceived already judged and rightfully condemned for this imputed sin (Rom. 5:15, 17; see also Jn. 3:18, 26; 1 Cor. 15:45-49; Eph. 2:3).

Jer. 19:4: "'Because they have forsaken Me and made this an alien place, because they have burned incense in it to other gods whom neither they, their fathers, nor the

---

[23] https://thecripplegate.com/what-happens-to-infants-who-die-the-ot-answers/

kings of Judah have known, and have filled this place with the blood of the innocents.'"

The argument goes that: "God refers to children in pagan families who are murdered as 'innocents' (Jer 19:4)...God does not throw around the term 'innocent' loosely (nor does he send 'innocent' people to hell)" (Ibid). But the term *innocent* is used quite often in the Old Testament in both a moral and/or legal sense. Deuteronomy 19, for instance, provides for capital punishment for murderers—of babies, those with profound IDD, and mature, responsible adults—in order to "put away the guilt of innocent blood" (vs. 13). Jonathan tries to persuade his father not to "sin against innocent blood" by killing David without cause (1 Sam. 19:5). And the Jewish kings were routinely condemned for killing innocent blood —babies, those with intellectual disabilities, and mature, responsible adults—without justification (2 Kings 21:16, 24:4; Jer. 2:34, 7:6, 22:3, 17, 26:15). So Jeremiah 19:4 is hardly proof of an age of innocence, but only that the slain were not deserving of being murdered.

Jonah 4:11: "'And should I not pity Nineveh, that great city, in which are more than one hundred and twenty thousand persons who cannot discern between their right hand and their left—and much livestock?'"

The argument from this passage states:

> God refers to Gentile children as unable to discern the difference between right and wrong (Jonah 4:11). Children are born with a sin nature, and even babies love to sin. But they do so without appreciating why they are doing it. Adults sin

because they discern what truth is, and have a disdain for it. Infants sin because they are unable to discern. There is a difference. (Ibid).

The problem with the argument is its horrible exegesis of the text. God is not saying that there are 120,000 inhabitants of Nineveh who have not yet reached the age of discernment. Rather, God is referring to the entire population of Nineveh, on whom He is bestowing mercy on despite their spiritual blindness. If ancient Babylon, the largest city in ancient Mesopotamia,[24] only had a population of 200,000 at its peak, then it clearly defies logic that Nineveh could have such a large population of just babies and those with profound IDD for that would be nearly all of its entire population!

1 Kings 14:12-13: "'12 Arise therefore, go to your own house. When your feet enter the city, the child shall die. 13 And all Israel shall mourn for him and bury him, for he is the only one of Jeroboam who shall come to the grave, because in him there is found something good toward the LORD God of Israel in the house of Jeroboam.'"

From this passage Pastor Johnson argues:

> He was an "innocent" infant, to borrow Jeremiah's language, and so he will still die, but will be spared the judicial punishment reserved for those who willingly revolted against God. Again, notice that in both this passage and in Jeremiah 19, God uses positive moral terms to apply to infants who die —

---

[24] https://en.wikipedia.org/wiki/Babylon

"innocent" and "good." Those are moral terms that God does not use willy-nilly. (Ibid.)

The Hebrew word that Johnson translates as *infant* is *yeled*, which is often translated as *boy* or *child* in the Old Testament. For instance, it is used in Genesis 21 to describe both the just-weaned Isaac (vs. 8) and his half-brother Ishmael (vs. 14-16), who was around the age of 14 at the time (compare Gen. 16:15-16 with Gen. 21:5). It is also used to describe all of Jacobs' then-eleven sons as he journeyed back to Canaan (Gen. 30:26, 32:22, 33:1-2, 5-7, 13-14).

Furthermore, in verse 3 of 1 Kings 14, the author uses the Hebrew word *naar* for the child, which is far more frequently translated as *young man* (see, for instance, Gen. 14:24, 18:7, 21:17-20, 22:3, 5, 12, 19, 25:27, 34:19; 1 Kings 3:7, 11:17, 28, 20:15, 17, 19). There is absolutely no warrant, therefore, to assume that Jeroboam's child was an infant. Nor is there any warrant to assume that this child did not have actual, genuine saving faith in Yahweh. The argument has no textual support whatsoever.

Is. 7:16: "'For before the Child shall know to refuse the evil and choose the good, the land that you dread will be forsaken by both her kings.'"

Pastor Johnson argues from this text that, "In other words, there is an age where children still sin, but not because of their knowledge of sin." Perhaps not because of their mature knowledge of sin do they sin, but because of their love for it they sin. This verse has nothing to do with an age of accountability, but simply demonstrates the sin nature of infants which have to be trained and disciplined to refuse the evil, which they naturally love, and choose to do good, which they naturally hate. We don't have to teach our children to do evil, but to do good (Deut. 21:18-21; Prov. 13:24, 20:30, 22:15, 23:131-5, 29:15).

3. A Mitigating Factor:

But while ignorance is no excuse, it may be a mitigating factor in determining eternal punishment. Scripture is clear, for instance, that we are accountable for what knowledge we do have. Jesus, for instance, warned the cities in which He had done most of His miracles that they would be judged far harsher for not repenting than those cities which had far less knowledge of Scriptural Truth:

> [20] Then He began to rebuke the cities in which most of His mighty works had been done, because they did not repent: [21] "Woe to you, Chorazin! Woe to you, Bethsaida! For if the mighty works which were done in you had been done in Tyre and Sidon, they would have repented long ago in sackcloth and ashes. [22] But I say to you, it will be more tolerable for Tyre and Sidon in the day of judgment than for you. [23] And you, Capernaum, who are exalted to heaven, will be brought down to Hades; for if the mighty works which were done in you had been done in Sodom, it would have remained until this day. [24] But I say to you that it shall be more tolerable for the land of Sodom in the day of judgment than for you."
> (Matt. 11:20-24; see also 10:15; Mk. 6:11; Lk. 12:47-48)

Jesus' reiterates this principle the night before His death:

> 22 If I had not come and spoken to them, they would have no sin, but now they have no excuse for their sin. 23 He who hates Me hates My Father also. 24 If I had not done among them the works which no one else did, they would have no sin; but now they have seen and also hated both Me and My Father. 25 But this happened that the word might be fulfilled which is written in their law, 'They hated Me without a cause.'
>
> (Jn. 15:22-25)

This is the reason why Jesus tells the Pharisees that they would be judged less severely if they had not seen the many signs which He performed among them (Jn. 9:41). But because, in their self-righteous pride they claimed to see and understand, their sin remains and abounds all the more (*Id.*).

John Piper engages in exegetical contortions when he attempts to argue from this passage in John 9 that Jesus is teaching that there is a category of blind people without sin before God. With all due respect to Piper, Jesus is saying no such thing in these verses:

> 39 And Jesus said, "For judgment I have come into this world, that those who do not see may see, and that those who see may be made blind."
> 40 Then some of the Pharisees who were with Him heard these words, and said to Him, "Are we blind also?"
> 41 Jesus said to them, "If you were blind, you would have no sin; but now you say, 'We see.' Therefore your sin remains.
>
> (Jn. 9:39-41)

For Piper knows full well that even if the Pharisees were blind in the John 9:41 sense of not having witnessed the signs (i.e., miracles) of Christ, they would still be with sin:

> But, in fact, you don't see. You are blind. And your guilt remains. Behind that little phrase, "you say that you see," is the profound statement of Jesus about our accountability: *In reality, they do not see. In reality, they are blind. And their guilt remains. And they are accountable.* (emphasis added)[25]

All of us, Piper admits, are blind and yet we remain guilty —accountable to a holy God for our sins. For all of us are sinners conceived blind (2 Cor. 4:3-4) and without any spiritual "capacity to see the revelation of God's will or God's glory"[26] and yet we remain guilty for our sins done in blindness. This is the default condition of every son of the First Man Adam (1 Cor. 2:14), and Jesus, in particular, regularly denounced the Pharisees as being blind (Matt. 23:16-17, 24. 26). And therefore, as Piper has argued elsewhere, the New Birth is needed for God to supernaturally open the eyes of the spiritually blind (2 Cor. 4:6):

> People who don't believe in Christ are blind. They can't see Christ as supremely valuable, and so they won't receive him as their Treasure and so they are not saved. A work of God is needed in their lives to open their eyes and give them life so

---

[25] https://www.desiringgod.org/messages/for-judgment-i-came-into-this-world

[26] https://www.desiringgod.org/articles/what-happens-to-infants-who-die

they can see and receive Christ as Savior and Lord and Treasure of their lives. That work of God is called new birth...According to 2 Corinthians 4, people are spiritually blind until God gives them eyes to see, that is, until God causes them to be born again.[27]

Finally, in returning to the argument that ignorance may be a mitigating factor in determining eternal punishment, we find that Scripture teaches us that hell will be proportionate to what each has done; in other words, "the punishment will fit the crime." Jesus states, for instance, that "He will reward each person according to what he has done" (Matt. 16:27). In the book of Revelation we read that, "The dead were judged according to what they had done as recorded in the books...each person was judged according to what he had done (Rev. 20:12-13; see also 2:23, 22:12). And the Apostle Paul tells us that, "God will give to each person according to what he has done" (Rom. 2:6; see also Ps. 62:12; Prov. 24:12; Ecc. 3:17; Jer. 32:19; Matt. 12:36-37; 2 Cor. 5:10).

Proponents of an age of accountability cite these passages, however, to argue that:

> Scripture teaches - and here's a summary statement I'm going to show you how it comes through Scripture, teaches that men and women are saved by what? Grace. But damned by works - by works. Scripture teaches that all condemned

---

[27] https://www.desiringgod.org/messages/im-sending-you-to-open-their-eyes

sinners earn their eternal punishment by their sins.[28]

These passages say no such thing; they only speak of proportional punishment and in no way contradict but merely compliment passages that clearly tell us that we are conceived as children of God's wrath.[29] Incidentally, just as these verses make no mention of the First Man Adam's sin and subsequent guilt as a grounds for eternal damnation, they also make no mention of faith as the instrumentality of eternal salvation. To be consistent, therefore, advocates of an age of accountability would have to say that these passages argue for both damnation and salvation by works and works alone.

In conclusion, while hell will be a place of unbearable torment for all of its prisoners, some will receive harsher punishment than others based on the degree of the hardness and unrepentantness of their hearts (Rom. 2:5; Heb. 10:29). Therefore, we can rest assured that though there may be babies and those with profound IDD in hell, their punishment will be far less severe than, say, Adolf Hitler or ever Mother Theresa.

CONCLUSION:

As we conclude this chapter, we have seen that universalism, Pelagianism, and an age of accountability have absolutely no Scriptural support. So we are still left in our dilemma, that babies and those with profound IDD are sin personified. That they themselves are sin, and their

---

[28] https://www.gty.org/library/sermons-library/80-242/the-salvation-of-babies-who-die-part-1

[29] Jn. 3:18, 26; Rom. 5:15, 17; 1 Cor. 15:45-49; Eph. 2:3

soul is black as night and uglier than hell. That they are as grotesque as any demon of hell from the moment of their conception. That they are:

- Unable to please God (Rom. 8:8).
- Unable to subject ourselves to the law of God (Rom. 8:7).
- At enmity with God (Jas. 4:4).
- Contrary to God (Gal. 5:17).
- With minds set on sin (Rom. 8:5; Phil. 3:19).
- Enemies of God (Rom. 5:10; Phil. 3:18; Jas. 4:4).

And that, therefore, they were conceived as children of wrath—spawns of Satan—under the rightful sentence of eternal damnation. God's wrath burns hot against them (Jn. 3:18, 36; Eph. 2:3) such that He cannot tolerate even their mere presence (Ps. 5:4-6, 7:11, 11:5). But even if He should let them into heaven, they would, like a infestation, pollute and defile His holy habitation by their mere presence (Num. 19:20; 1 Cor. 3:17). Furthermore, even their own parents and siblings would, out of perfect love for all that is perfectly holy, cast them into hell should God give them leave. And finally, even they themselves would hate both God and their family with such loathing that they would consider heaven hell and seek by whatever desperate means to escape, even if that meant actually going to hell.

So is there any solution to this dilemma?

7 EXAMINING OTHER PROOF TEXTS

*I*n this chapter we will examine several other arguments and proof texts used to support the belief that at least some babies and those with profound IDD go to heaven.

Ezek. 16:21: "'that you have slain My children and offered them up to them by causing them to pass through the fire?'"

The argument goes as follows:

> Infants belong to God in a special and particular way. In Ezekiel, God describes the slaughter of children born into pagan families as a slaughter of "my children" (Ezek 16:21). This expression of ownership by God over children born into idol worshiping families is stark, and implies God's care for those children in a personal way.[1]

The implications of such an argument for the fatherhood of God of all mankind—a proposition flatly denied by Scripture—is quite problematic. But in this passage God is rebuking the Jewish people for committing harlotry with what He had given them—"My gold and My silver, which I have given you" (vs. 17), "My oil and My incense" (vs. 18), and "My food which I gave you" (vs. 19). So far from showing "care" in a "personal way," God is emphasizing the heinousness of their idolatry by misappropriating His good gifts.

---

[1] https://thecripplegate.com/what-happens-to-infants-who-die-the-ot-answers/

Children of Believers Saved?:

Are babies and children with profound IIDD of believers automatically saved because they are within the covenant of God? Many of those denominations that practice infant baptism believe so, holding that all children who have at least one believing parent go to heaven. Don't bother, however, looking for a chapter and verse to support that.

We do know, for instance, that God does, at times, save the children of those who trust Him. God saved Noah's children, for instance, from the Flood, "because I have seen that you are righteous before Me in this generation" (Gen. 7:1; see also Heb. 11:7). When God destroyed Sodom and Gomorrah, He spared Lot and his family because, "God remembered Abraham" (Gen. 19:29). We also have verses that, generally speaking, show God extending mercy to the children of His children (Ps. 103:17; 112:1-2, 115:14-15; Prov. 20:7).

But we also know from the examples of Cain, Esau, and Absalom that not every child of believers grows up to love the Lord. And certainly if countless Christians throughout the ages have had unbelieving adult children, then it stands to reason that they may also have had unbelieving babies and children with profound IDD as well. Elect parents do not automatically beget elect children and grandchildren—whether within the womb or out, whether with mental and physical disabilities or without.

And therefore it is impossible to say that babies and children with profound IDD of believers are automatically entitled to heaven upon death. Consequently, the Canons of Dort goes too far when it says, "godly parents ought not to doubt the election and salvation of their children whom God calls out of this life in infancy." Such a claim is entirely without Scriptural warrant.

Does Infant Baptism Save?:

There are certain heretical cults of the Christian faith that believe in baptismal regeneration—the false doctrine that one is born again through the sacrament of baptism. Not through faith alone, but through works divorced from any actual, genuine saving faith at all. Which is why they baptize infants, in order to punch their ticket to heaven before they might die at an early age. In reality, however, this teaching has had the opposite effect, deluding billions into hell all while thinking that a mere sprinkling of water once upon a time saved them.

For instance, Part 2 of section 2 of Chapter 1 of Article 1, paragraph 1213, of the Roman Catholic Catechism, reads:

> Holy Baptism is the basis of the whole Christian life, the gateway to life in the Spirit, and the door which gives access to the other sacraments. Through Baptism we are freed from sin and reborn as sons of God; we become members of Christ, are incorporated into the Church and made sharers in her mission: "Baptism is the sacrament of regeneration through water in the word."

Similarly, the Lutheran catechism states that, "Baptism worketh forgiveness of sins, delivers from death and the devil, and gives everlasting salvation to all who believe as the Word of the promise of God declare." And the Lutheran Augsburg Confession claims:

> Of Baptism they teach that it is necessary to salvation, and that through Baptism is offered the grace of God, and that children are to be baptized

who by baptism being offered to God are received into God's favor.

This is one of the most dangerous, false, heretical teachings that, unfortunately, far too many professing Christians believe, base their assurance of salvation on, and indoctrinate others with. Why do I say that? Because, among other things, it isn't warranted by Scripture.

The **first** primary text they cite for their heretical teaching is John 3:5: "Jesus answered, 'Most assuredly, I say to you, unless one is born of water and the Spirit, he cannot enter the kingdom of God.'" The term *born of water* here does not mean *baptism*. This is the only place in Scripture in which the phrase *born of water* is used. The phrase *of water* is used twenty-nine times in the New Testament, none of which are in reference to baptism. There is a Greek word for baptism, *baptizo*, which means submerge or immersion and is used over one-hundred times in the New Testament in various tenses.

Secondly, the phrase *born of water* is not used again in John, chapter 3, which is highly unusual if Christ were, in fact, teaching baptismal regeneration. Instead, however, only faith is stressed repeatedly as the prerequisite for salvation:

- **Vs. 15:** "Whoever *believes* in Him should not perish but have eternal life" (emphasis added).
- **Vs. 16:** "Whoever *believes* in HIm should not perish but have everlasting life" (emphasis added).
- **Vs. 18:** "Whoever *believes* in Him is not condemned, but he who does not *believe* is condemned already..." (emphasis added).

In short, baptismal regeneration denies faith alone by grace alone and replaces it with works, in clear violation of Scriptural teaching:

- **Romans 11:6**: "...if by grace, then it is no longer of works; if it were, grace would no longer be grace."
- **Eph. 2:8:** "it is by grace you have been saved through faith—and this not of yourselves, it is a gift of God—not of works so that no one can boast."
- **Rom. 3:27-28:** "[27] Where then is boasting? It is excluded. On what principle? On that of observing the law? No, but on that of faith. [28] For we maintain that a man is justified by faith apart from observing the law." (see also Gal. 2:16; 3:11)

Third, baptismal regeneration is entirely incompatible with the wind analogy of verse 8 of John 3: "'The Spirit blows where He wills, and you hear His voice, but you have not known where He comes and where He goes. Thus is everyone who has been born of the Spirit.'" Doing an act—whether baptism or any other—in order to earn one's salvation (or that of their infant child) is completely opposed to Christ's teaching that salvation is by the sovereign will of God and God alone. The Spirit cannot be manipulated by man's will—whether by making a decision, saying a "sinner's prayer," partaking of the sacraments, etc.—but solely blows where He wishes:

- **John 1:12-13:** "[12] But as many as received Him, to them He gave the right to become children of God, to those who believe in His name, [13] who were born, not of blood, nor of the will of the flesh, nor of the will of man, but of God."

- **Romans 9:16:** "So then it is not of him who wills nor of him who runs, but of God who shows mercy."

In short, baptismal regeneration denies God's sovereign grace alone, and it thereby denies God the praise and worship due His name and His name alone (Eph. 1:6, 12, 14).

And the fourth and final reason for why the phrase *born of water* cannot mean baptismal regeneration is that Nicodemus would not have known about baptism from the Old Testament. So what does it matter, you might be thinking to yourself, what Nicodemus knew and didn't know. Because Jesus thought it mattered, for in verse 10 we read: "'Jesus answered and said to him, 'Are you the teacher of Israel, and *do not know these things*?'" (emphasis added). In other words, Jesus expected Nicodemus to know from the Old Testament what He was talking about when He used the phrase *born of water*. But there is nothing in the Old Testament about baptism, which was not introduced until the ministry of John the Baptist. So it is impossible that Nicodemus would have understood from the Old Testament that the phrase *born of water* referred to baptism, and therefore either Jesus is wrong or Catholics and Lutherans are wrong.

The **second** text they point to comes from the third chapter of Peter's first epistle:

> [18] For Christ also suffered once for sins, the just for the unjust, that He might bring us to God, being put to death in the flesh but made alive by the Spirit, [19] by whom also He went and preached to the spirits in prison, [20] who formerly were disobedient, when once the Divine longsuffering

waited in the days of Noah, while the ark was being prepared, in which a few, that is, eight souls, were saved through water. 21 There is also an antitype which now saves us—baptism (not the removal of the filth of the flesh, but the answer of a good conscience toward God), through the resurrection of Jesus Christ, 22 who has gone into heaven and is at the right hand of God, angels and authorities and powers having been made subject to Him.

(1 Pet. 3:18-22)

Their argument from this passage suffers from flaws number two and three that we just looked at in examining John 3:5. But look at what Peter is saying in verse 21. He specifically says that water baptism, though it may remove bodily filth, does *not* save us. Rather, the resurrection of Jesus Christ, like Noah's Ark, saves from destruction. And this salvation—this ark—is ours if we have a good conscience toward God that is pledged or professed[2] by the ordinance of baptism, which symbolically represents our unification by *faith* in the death and resurrection of Christ.

We find a nearly parallel passage from the Apostle Paul in the second chapter of Colossians:

---

[2] The Greek word translated here by the NKJV for *answer* is *eperotema*, which is an extremely rare Greek word only used here in the New Testament. It may mean *inquiry*, *request*, *appeal*, *demand*, a *profession*, or *pledge*, depending on the context. Paul uses a similar phraseology in context of a good conscience in Rom. 9:1 ("my conscience also bearing me witness") and 2 Cor. 1:12 ("the testimony of our conscience").

> [11] In Him you were also circumcised with the circumcision made without hands, by putting off the body of the sins of the flesh, by the circumcision of Christ, [12] buried with Him in baptism, in which you also were raised with Him through faith in the working of God, who raised Him from the dead. [13] And you, being dead in your trespasses and the uncircumcision of your flesh, He has made alive together with Him, having forgiven you all trespasses, [14] having wiped out the handwriting of requirements that was against us, which was contrary to us. And He has taken it out of the way, having nailed it to the cross. [15] Having disarmed principalities and powers, He made a public spectacle of them, triumphing over them in it.
>
> (Col. 2:11-15)

We, who once were "dead in our trespasses and the uncircumcision of our flesh" (vs. 13), have now, died to the "body of the sins of the flesh" (vs. 11). This spiritual union with Christ is symbolized by baptism (vs. 12). And our new life in Christ is also symbolized by our rising out of the waters of baptism (vs. 12). And this spiritual union with Christ is only by the instrumentality of faith (vs. 12), without which any symbolic union has no meaning. And like 1 Peter 3, this passage from Colossians 2 concludes with the triumph of Christ over all His enemies.

In short, there is absolutely no Scriptural support for the heresy that baptism saves anyone—baby, those with profound IDDs, or a mature, responsible adult.

2 Samuel 12:23:

Many who argue that babies go to heaven point to the twelfth chapter of 2 Samuel, where King David's infant son had just perished due to his adultery with Bathsheba and (indirect) murder of her husband. David's attendants were wondering why, upon learning of the child's death, he had stopped fasting. David explains that he fasted while the child was alive in hopes that God would show mercy to him (2 Sam. 12:22). "But now he is dead, why should I fast? Can I bring him back again? I shall go to him, but he shall not return to me" (vs. 23).

Many read that and think, "Since David is an Old Testament saint after God's own heart and therefore is going to heaven, the only way he will be going to his son is if the baby is also in heaven. Ergo, if David's baby is in heaven, my baby must also in heaven." That's a grossly unstable theorem built upon a shaky pile of assumptions that is nowhere found in the text itself.

David is simply referring to the grave. The general holding place of the dead, often called *Sheol* in the Old Testament. And there is nothing particularly unique about David's phraseology. For instance, from the grave the prophet Samuel told David's predecessor King Saul that, "tomorrow you and your sons will be with me" (1 Sam. 28:19). Now by all accounts, King Saul and at least some of his sons died in their sins without penitent faith and are even now in flames of torment (2 Sam. 21:1). But there is absolutely no indication in Scripture that that is Samuel's fate. So Samuel could not have possibly meant that Saul and all of his sons would be exactly where he was enjoying peace and plenty.

Furthermore, over and over in the Old Testament we read the phrase that so-and-so died and "rested with his fathers" (1 Kings 2:10, 11:43; et. al.). This, again, can only refer to a general holding facility of the dead rather than a statement of eternal fates, for the fathers of these individuals were a mixed bag—some righteous and some unrighteous—that therefore, of necessity, must have different eternal destinies such that their progeny could not possibly rest simultaneously with them in two separate locations.

Ecc. 6:3-6:

> 3 If a man begets a hundred children and lives many years, so that the days of his years are many, but his soul is not satisfied with goodness, or indeed he has no burial, I say that a stillborn child is better than he— 4 for it comes in vanity and departs in darkness, and its name is covered with darkness. 5 Though it has not seen the sun or known anything, this has more rest than that man, 6 even if he lives a thousand years twice—but has not seen goodness. Do not all go to one place?
> (Ecc. 6:3-6)

Though it doesn't change the meaning, the Hebrew word for *stillborn* used in verse 3 is *nephel*, which literally means *to fall*. The King James translates it as an *untimely birth*, and the Hebrew can refer to either a *miscarriage* or *stillbirth*.

Solomon, the preacher of Ecclesiastes, isn't saying here that a child of untimely birth is in heaven. Rather, he is simply using an analogy—that it would have been better never to have "seen the sun or known anything" (vs. 5) than to live a thousand years twice (vs. 6) without once having satisfied one's soul with goodness (vs. 3). Nothing more, and nothing less. And he isn't saying that a stillborn has rest *in heaven*, only that he has *more rest* than such a man who actually lived but never seen goodness.

He says something similar two chapters earlier:

> [1] Then I returned and considered all the oppression that is done under the sun:
> And look! The tears of the oppressed,
> But they have no comforter—
> On the side of their oppressors there is power,
> But they have no comforter.
> [2] Therefore I praised the dead who were already dead,
> More than the living who are still alive.
> [3] Yet, better than both is he who has never existed,
> Who has not seen the evil work that is done under the sun.
>
> (Ecc. 4:1-3)

Better is it to be stillborn, better is it to have never existed, then to see "the evil work that is done under the sun" (vs. 3). Again, it is a mere analogy and not to be taken as a definite statement on the eternal state of babies and those with profound IDD.

Job 3:1-19:

> [1] After this Job opened his mouth and cursed the day of his birth. [2] And Job spoke, and said:
> [3] "May the day perish on which I was born,
> And the night in which it was said,
> 'A male child is conceived.'

⁴ May that day be darkness;
May God above not seek it,
Nor the light shine upon it.
⁵ May darkness and the shadow of death claim it;
May a cloud settle on it;
May the blackness of the day terrify it.
⁶ As for that night, may darkness seize it;
May it not rejoice among the days of the year,
May it not come into the number of the months.
⁷ Oh, may that night be barren!
May no joyful shout come into it!
⁸ May those curse it who curse the day,
Those who are ready to arouse Leviathan.
⁹ May the stars of its morning be dark;
May it look for light, but have none,
And not see the dawning of the day;
¹⁰ Because it did not shut up the doors of my mother's womb,
Nor hide sorrow from my eyes.
¹¹ "Why did I not die at birth?
Why did I not perish when I came from the womb?
¹² Why did the knees receive me?
Or why the breasts, that I should nurse?
¹³ For now I would have lain still and been quiet,
I would have been asleep;
Then I would have been at rest
¹⁴ With kings and counselors of the earth,
Who built ruins for themselves,
¹⁵ Or with princes who had gold,
Who filled their houses with silver;
¹⁶ Or why was I not hidden like a stillborn child,
Like infants who never saw light?
¹⁷ There the wicked cease from troubling,
And there the weary are at rest.

> [18] There the prisoners rest together;
> They do not hear the voice of the oppressor.
> [19] The small and great are there,
> And the servant is free from his master.
>
> (Job 3:1-19)

Proponents argue that this passage shows that stillborn children go to heaven because, so the argument goes, why would Job long to be a stillborn child if infants and those with profound IDD go to hell. Job says much the same thing in the tenth chapter of Job:

> [14] If I sin, then You mark me,
> And will not acquit me of my iniquity.
> [15] If I am wicked, woe to me;
> Even if I am righteous, I cannot lift up my head.
> I am full of disgrace;
> See my misery!
> [16] If my head is exalted,
> You hunt me like a fierce lion,
> And again You show Yourself awesome against me.
> [17] You renew Your witnesses against me,
> And increase Your indignation toward me;
> Changes and war are ever with me.
> [18] 'Why then have You brought me out of the womb?
> Oh, that I had perished and no eye had seen me!
> [19] I would have been as though I had not been.
> I would have been carried from the womb to the grave.
> [20] Are not my days few?
> Cease! Leave me alone, that I may take a little comfort,

²¹ Before I go to the place from which I shall not return,
To the land of darkness and the shadow of death,
²² A land as dark as darkness itself,
As the shadow of death, without any order,
Where even the light is like darkness.'"
(Job 10:14-19)

We must keep the story of Job in context. Job is a man in so much pain and torment that we can't even fathom it. He lost all his livestock (1:13-17). His children all died in a single natural calamity (1:18-19). He has "painful boils from the sole of his foot to the crown of his head" (2:7). His wife wants him to curse God so he would die and be put out of his misery (2:9). His three "friends" wrongfully accuse him of wrongdoing. And in perhaps the greatest understatement of the Bible, we are told that Job's "grief was very great" (2:13). And this has been Job's lot for months on end (7:3).

Job just wanted to die or, better yet in his eyes, to have never been born and lived to see such agony and suffering in the first place. In fact, his faith begins to waver with each passing hour of absolute misery:

¹⁸ "But as a mountain falls and crumbles away,
And as a rock is moved from its place;
¹⁹ As water wears away stones,
And as torrents wash away the soil of the earth;
So You destroy the hope of man.
²⁰ You prevail forever against him, and he passes on;
You change his countenance and send him away.
(Job 14:18-20)

He even casts doubt upon heaven and a bodily resurrection (though he later rebounds in 19:25-27):

> [7] "For there is hope for a tree,
> If it is cut down, that it will sprout again,
> And that its tender shoots will not cease.
> [8] Though its root may grow old in the earth,
> And its stump may die in the ground,
> [9] Yet at the scent of water it will bud
> And bring forth branches like a plant.
> [10] But man dies and is laid away;
> Indeed he breathes his last
> And where is he?...
> [14] If a man dies, shall he live again?...
> (Job 14:7-10, 14a)

The point is that we should be very cautious with attributing to Job a desire to have been a stillborn babe (3:1-19) because that meant he would have been in heaven. This was a man who merely wanted to be put out of his misery or, better yet, never in such misery to begin with. He isn't engaged in a definitive statement on the eternal state of babies and those with profound IDD. He's simply longing for death. There is much good in what Job says, but not all of what he says is Gospel truth.

As Jon Bloom, cofounder of Desiring God, wrote:

> "The dead are better off than I am and I wish I'd never been born." There's not much gospel in that perspective. There's no expressed gratitude for prior blessings, or faith that God might have higher, hidden purposes that someday would work for a yet unknown good. Just horror.

Did these words accurately represent Job's deepest beliefs? No. Like David in Psalm 22:1 and Heman the Ezrahite in Psalm 88:14, Job's words were shrieks of pain. Like the puss of infection oozing from the sores on Job's body (Job 2:7–8), words of desolation were oozing from the sores on his soul.[3]

Salvation After Death:

The Bible is unequivocally clear that there is no salvation after death, for "it is appointed for men to die once, but after this the judgment" (Heb. 9:27). And in the parable of Lazarus and the rich man in the sixteenth chapter of Luke, we are told in verses 22-23 that hell is the immediate destination of the unregenerate upon death. For this rich man died (vs. 22) and, immediately (vs. 23), he was in hell. Not the next day. Not the next hour. Not even a second later. But immediately, simultaneously with death, he was in hell. He knew he was in hell long before his family and friends knew he was even dead. There was no chance to turn around. No chance to repent. No chance to say, "I'm sorry!" No! Immediately upon his last breath his eternal fate was sealed forever.

But, furthermore, we find that hell is inescapable in terms of *location*. For verse 26 tells us that a great chasm is fixed between heaven and hell over which no one can pass. The original Greek word for *fixed* is even stronger, indicating that the chasm is *set fast*, *securely established*. In other words, it is immovable. It is unfailing. It is

---

[3] https://www.desiringgod.org/articles/how-to-be-a-miserable-comforter

unyielding. No one ever has or will escape from it. Ever. No one crosses over from hell to heaven. No one.

But we also see that hell is inescapable in terms of *duration*. For Jesus describes hell as a "'fire that *shall never be quenched*, where their worm *never dies*'" (Mk. 9:44, 46, 48; emphasis added). And the book of Revelation warns us that, "the smoke of their torment [will] ascend *forever and ever*, and they will have *no rest day or night*" (14:11).

There is no second chance after death. There are no do-overs. No reincarnation. No reprieve. No clemency. No stint in purgatory to make amends. The chance for repentance is over and the sentence is fixed forever upon one's final breath (Lk. 16:26; Rev. 20:11-15). Hell is truth realized too late. The only thing annihilated in hell is hope.

The English Puritan preacher Thomas Watson illustrated the eternity of hell this way:

> Oh eternity! If all the body of earth and sea were turned to sand, and all the air up to the starry heaven were nothing but sand, and a little bird should come every thousand years, and fetch away in her bill but the tenth part of a grain of all that heap of sand, what numberless years would be spent before that vast heap of sand would be fetched away!
>
> Yet, if at the end of all that time, the sinner might come out of hell, there would be some hope; but that word "Ever" breaks the heart. "The smoke of their torment ascendeth up for ever and ever."

Or as Dante puts it in his play *Divine Comedy*:

> Through me you pass into the city of woe:
> Through me you pass into eternal pain:
> Through me among the people lost for aye.
> Justice the founder of my fabric moved:
> To rear me was the task of power divine,
> Supremest wisdom, and primeval love.
> Before me things create were none, save things
> Eternal, and eternal I shall endure.
> All hope abandon, ye who enter here.

Despite the complete lack of Scriptural support—nay, in fact, the entirety of Scriptural evidence to the contrary—John Piper speculates that babies and those with profound IDD might be saved after death:

> So I am leaving open the possibility that in some way that I do not know and don't want to speculate too far about, God might be pleased to make that possible for them to come to faith after death.[4]

Again, in another place, he argues:

> It seems to me that the most natural guess would be that babies will grow up in the kingdom (either immediately, or over time) and will by God's grace come to faith so that their justification is by faith alone just like ours.[5]

---

[4] https://www.desiringgod.org/interviews/can-a-sinner-be-saved-after-death

[5] https://www.desiringgod.org/articles/what-happens-to-infants-who-die

When Scripture is silent, we do not speak. And when Scripture is against us, we repent and change our views. Such statements by Piper are grossly irresponsible.

Matthew 19:13-15:

Many also cite the following passage as a reason to believe that all babies (and presumably those with profound IDD) are in heaven:

> 13 Then little children were brought to Him that He might put His hands on them and pray, but the disciples rebuked them. 14 But Jesus said, "Let the little children come to Me, and do not forbid them; for of such is the kingdom of heaven." 15 And He laid His hands on them and departed from there.
> (Matt. 19:13-15; see also Mk. 10:13-16; Lk. 18:15-17)

However, Jesus is not saying here that babies are in heaven. For one thing, if that is what He is saying, the statement would literally mean that the kingdom of heaven is *only* made up of babies and no others: "Do not forbid them for such is the kingdom of heaven." But that isn't what Christ said. Secondly, the Greek word for *little children* (*paidion*) is not exclusive to babies or even infants, but encompasses older children as well (see, for instance, Matt. 14:21, 15:38). Older children, mind you, that likely already reached the "age of accountability."

Third and most importantly, Jesus is making an analogy in this passage—that unless you come to Christ with childlike faith, you will not enter the kingdom of heaven (Matt. 18:3). Hence the phrase *of such* indicates that the inhabitants of heaven are like unto—similar but not equal to—children. For a similar usage, we find in the eighteenth chapter of Matthew that Jesus uses the phrase *little ones* repeatedly in reference to disciples (see also Matt. 10:42, 11:25; Mk. 9:37, 9:41-42, 10:29; Lk. 17:1-4). Therefore, the kingdom of God is no more made up of babies than it is of good seed (Matt. 13:38), hidden treasure (vs. 44), pearls of great price (vs. 45-46), and good fish (vs. 47-50). These are analogies of the real thing; not literally the real thing.

Revelation 5:9: "And they sang a new song, saying: 'You are worthy to take the scroll and to open its seals: for You were slain and have redeemed us to God by Your blood out of every tribe and tongue and people and nation'" (see also Rev. 7:9-10).

So, Pastor Johnson argues, "Because so many languages and tribes have died out, this is only feasible through the salvation of infants."[6] Unfortunately, Johnson doesn't explain why, textually, this could be accomplished only through the salvation of babies and those with profound IDD in ages past rather than through the salvation of mature, responsible adults in ages past. Or by the spontaneous regeneration of extinct tribes, tongues, and people groups. His argument only works if babies and those with profound IDD are innocent under the theory of an age of accountability. But as has been demonstrated exhaustively in this book, there is no such thing and, consequently, his argument holds no water.

Additionally, the phrase "every tribe and tongue and people and nation"—which is exhaustively duplicative—is used with minor variations in a number of other places in

---

[6] https://thecripplegate.com/what-happens-to-infants-who-die-the-nt-answers/

the book of Revelation (10:11, 11:9, 13:7, 14:6, 17:15). The reason the phrase is repetitive is simple—to be sweepingly comprehensive but, much like the word *world* in John 3:17 and *all* in John 12:32, not *necessarily* entirely all-inclusive.

Furthermore it appears to refer to those peoples currently on the earth. In Revelation 14:6, for instance, we read of a flying angel who preaches "the everlasting gospel" to, "those who dwell on the earth—to every nation, tribe, tongue, and people." Surely that angel was not time traveling, but heralding the Gospel to those who currently inhabit the earth. Or, for example, only present-time "peoples, multitudes, nations, and tongues" (17:15) will give their kingdoms to the beast and wage war with the Lamb, not extinct ethnic groups brought back to life. So, too, the phrase in Revelation 5:9 and 7:9 likely only refers to current tribes, tongues, peoples, and nations, not to all who ever existed.

CONCLUSION:

As we conclude this chapter, we have seen that, so far, there is absolutely no Scriptural support that babies and those with profound IDD are in heaven, despite the vast number of arguments put forward by proponents. So we are still left in our dilemma, that these individuals, as all the sons of the First Man Adam, are sin personified. That they themselves are sin, and their soul is black as night and uglier than hell. That they are as grotesque as any demon of hell from the moment of their conception. That they are:

- Unable to please God (Rom. 8:8).
- Unable to subject ourselves to the law of God (Rom. 8:7).

- At enmity with God (Jas. 4:4).
- Contrary to God (Gal. 5:17).
- With minds set on sin (Rom. 8:5; Phil. 3:19).
- Enemies of God (Rom. 5:10; Phil. 3:18; Jas. 4:4).

And that, therefore, they were conceived as children of wrath—spawns of Satan—under the rightful sentence of eternal damnation. God's wrath burns hot against them (Jn. 3:18, 36; Eph. 2:3) such that He cannot tolerate even their mere presence (Ps. 5:4-6, 7:11, 11:5). But even if He should let them into heaven, they would, like a infestation, pollute and defile His holy habitation by their mere presence (Num. 19:20; 1 Cor. 3:17). Furthermore, even their own parents and siblings would, out of perfect love for all that is perfectly holy, cast them into hell should God give them leave. And finally, even they themselves would hate both God and their family with such loathing that they would consider heaven hell and seek by whatever desperate means to escape, even if that meant actually going to hell.

So is there any solution to this dilemma?

8 HOW, THEN, CAN THEY BE SAVED?

How, then, can babies and those with profound IDD be saved? Is there any hope for them? How is it possible that a holy and righteous God save those unable to respond to the Gospel message? For Romans is clear that penitent faith—the only instrument by which one is saved—comes only through the word of God (Rom. 10:17). So how can a baby or those with profound IDD hear, understand, and respond to Scripture? Isn't it impossible?

Indeed it is. But then, so too would a baby being filled with the Holy Spirit while in his mother's womb (Lk. 1:15). And it would be impossible for an unborn child to recognize the voice of the mother of his Savior and leap for joy (vs. 44). And it would be impossible for an unborn child to testify that God has been his God from his mother's womb (Ps. 22:10), and that he learned to trust God while still nursing (vs. 9). And it would be impossible for an unborn child to be sanctified by God (Jer. 1:5).

But these things did happen, and therefore these examples appear to leave the door open to an exception to the ordinary *order salutis* (order of salvation)—effectual calling via hearing the Word, regeneration/new birth, penitent faith, justification, adoption, and glorification. And if there were three regenerated unborn babies in Scripture, it stands to reason that there could, *theoretically*, be more. That God's sovereign electing grace is not *always* limited by Romans 10:17. Most of the time, yes. 99.9% of the time, absolutely. But in the case of mental and physical inability to understand God's truth, God *may* sovereignly intervene. There is nothing in Scripture that guarantees or mandates such an intervention of sovereign grace, but neither is it foreclosed.

We are all but clay in the hands of the Potter, who prepared some of us beforehand for eternal wrath and others for eternal glory (Rom. 9:22-23). Of His own free and independent will, God alone decides whom He will show mercy to and whom He will harden (vs. 18). Therefore, it is not of him who wills nor of him who runs, but of God who shows mercy (vs. 16). And God is certainly capable of effectuating His electing purposes to babies and those with profound IDD, and nothing, including physical and mental limitations, can thwart His hand.

So paragraph 3 of Chapter 10 of the 1689 Second London Baptist Confession of Faith is correct, so far as it goes, in stating:

> Elect infants dying in infancy are regenerated and saved by Christ through the Spirit; who works when, and where, and how He pleases; so also are all elect persons, who are incapable of being outwardly called by the ministry of the Word

The Confession is absolutely correct in stressing the need for regeneration and justification through the completed work of Christ by the work of the Holy Spirit. There are three elect unborn babies in the Bible we know this was true of, which means it could be true of many more as well.

But beyond this we cannot speculate, much less say with any degree of certainty. As Professor Wayne Grudem notes in his Systematic Theology:

> How many infants does God save in this way? Scripture does not tell us, so we simply cannot know. Where Scripture is silent, it is unwise for us to make definitive pronouncements.

Like Dutch theologian Herman Bavink, we have to confess, "I would not wish to deny, nor am I able to affirm" infant salvation. Or with Professor Cornelius Venema, "caution is preferable to the confident denial or affirmation of this possibility."

But perhaps we are asking the wrong question. Rather than asking whether babies (born and unborn) and those with profound IDD go to heaven, we should be asking ourselves whether we trust the Potter to act with perfect and infinite wisdom, goodness, love, and righteousness. As we "suffer[] according to the will of God," have we committed ourselves to Him as to "a faithful Creator" (1 Pet. 4:19)? Have we left it in God's hands, for the Judge of all the earth shall do right (Gen. 18:25)? Perhaps there is no greater test of one's view of God than this.

Some may argue that there is no comfort, no peace, in such a perspective. They want definitive answers as a rock for their hope. But the doctrine of sovereign grace is exactly that kind of comfort. Nay, it is the best kind of comfort imaginable. Look at how Jonathan Edwards describes his new attitude toward the doctrine of election:

> But I have often, since that first conviction, had quite another kind of sense of God's sovereignty than I had then. I have often since had not only a conviction, but a delightful conviction. The doctrine has very often appeared exceedingly pleasant, bright and sweet. Absolute sovereignty is what I love to ascribe to God.

O, what a "delightful conviction" it is! What an "exceedingly pleasant, bright and sweet" doctrine! For without it I have absolutely no hope that my babies are in heaven. For those who deny sovereign grace in favor of man's free will—that he must provide the decisive ingredient of penitent faith to save himself— have no hope for the salvation of babies and those with profound IDD. For if God cannot sovereignly, unilaterally, monogestically make one a believer after birth, He cannot do so before birth. If He cannot violate man's "free will" after birth, then He cannot do so before birth. But thanks be to God that He has that power, which He exercises perfectly for the maximization of our eternal joy in the maximization of His glory! O!—that we serve a God so free, sovereign, and independent in all that He does, for only such a God is worth worshipping!

So let the clay—which has no rights—silence our complaining and grumbling against the Potter (Is. 29:16, 45:9; Rom. 9:20). Let us stop running from and hiding from such a God as this that we become woefully inconsistent and contradictory in our interpretation of Scripture. Rather, let us praise the Lord for His untraceable ways and unfathomable mercy in His absolutely and infinitely perfect, wise, good, and righteous election of His children:

> [33] Oh, the depth of the riches both of the wisdom and knowledge of God! How unsearchable are His judgments and His ways past finding out!
> [34] "For who has known the mind of the Lord?
> Or who has become His counselor?"
> [35] "Or who has first given to Him
> And it shall be repaid to him?"
> [36] For of Him and through Him and to Him are all things, to whom be glory forever. Amen.
> (Rom. 11:33-36)

Such God-centered, man-debasing worship is the Gospel in full-bloom (Is. 64:8)!

Nathan W. Tucker

IT IS WELL WITH MY SOUL
By Horatio G. Spatford

1 When peace like a river attendeth my way,
When sorrows like sea billows roll;
Whatever my lot Thou hast taught me to say,
"It is well, it is well with my soul!"

Chorus: It is well with my soul!
It is well, it is well with my soul!

2 Though Satan should buffet, though trials should come,
Let this blest assurance control,
That Christ hath regarded my helpless estate,
And hath shed His own blood for my soul.

3 My sin—oh, the bliss of this glorious thought—
My sin, not in part, but the whole,
Is nailed to His Cross, and I bear it no more;
Praise the Lord, praise the Lord, O my soul!

4 For me, be it Christ, be it Christ hence to live;
If dark hours about me shall roll,
No pang shall be mine, for in death as in life
Thou wilt whisper Thy peace to my soul.

9 GOD ALONE IS ENOUGH

*I*n the span of slightly over three years, I buried both my parents to terminal illnesses as well as suffered the loss of five miscarried children. I speak from a heart that daily grieves. The missing chairs around the table make the holidays incredibly lonely. Visions of Christmases past as well as Christmases that Will Never Be haunt what should otherwise be a joyous time of the year. The question *why* continually plagues our thoughts and prayers.

Unfortunately, we will find few, if any, answers this side of eternity. I know that there are dark nights of the soul when, like Job, the shrieks of pain continually ooze from our desolate hearts that no salve can treat. There are no pat answers. At times all we can do is cry out to God, "I believe, help my unbelief!" (Mk. 9:24). I have by no means arrived (Phil. 3:12), but am still in the valley struggling. However, I wish to share with you the comfort with which I have been comforted by God (2 Cor. 1:4).

The rest for my soul, the anchor of my faith, is not the eternal fate of my babies. Not in the least. Rather, my hope lies in Christ and Christ alone. Christ is my heaven, whether in life or in death.

As my wife has put it:

> I know that my babies may not be in heaven. They might not be part of the elect, and it breaks my heart. But while I am on this earth, I find it comforting to think that I will see them again. And when it comes time for all believers to be with Him in eternity, and my babies are not there, I will have no tears, for my heart will be filled with immense joy to be face-to-face with my Savior!

Christ is Our All:

In chapter 1 of Philippians we find the Apostle Paul describing Christ as treasure in both life and death:

> [19] For I have known that this shall fall out to me for salvation, through your heartfelt petition and the supply of the Spirit of Messiah Jesus, [20] according to my earnest expectation and hope that in nothing I shall be ashamed, but in all boldness, as always, so also now Messiah shall be magnified in my body, whether through life or through death. [21] for to me to live is Messiah, and to die gain. [22] But if I live on in the flesh, it is to me the fruit of work. But then what shall I choose I know not. [23] For I am pressed by the two, having the desire to depart and to be with Messiah, for it is far better. [24] But to remain in the flesh is more necessary on your account.
>
> (Phil. 1:19-24 NYLT)

For a number of years while living in Iowa I had PHIL121 as my license plate; it is easily one of my two favorite verses (the other being Galatians 2:20). Look with me first at verse 20, where Paul states that his earnest expectation and hope—his single-minded desire—is that Christ would be magnified in his body. The Greek word translated here as *magnify* (megaluno) means "to make or declare great." It is translated in other verses as *enlarge*, *exalt*, or *displaying greatness*. In other words, Paul wants Christ to be made much of—whether by his life or his death.

And then look at verse 21, where Paul tells us how Christ will be magnified in his life—"for to me, to live is Messiah, and to die gain." Let's focus on that last part first.

Death is Gain. How does Paul say that Christ will be magnified in his death? Because death is gain. But how in the world could the Apostle Paul tell us that death is gain? Death is the final goodbye. It is goodbye to a beloved spouse. Can you imagine telling your precious sweetheart of 50 years that you love them, but that death will be even better? It is goodbye to children, grandchildren, and great-grandchildren. It is goodbye to a great, fulfilling career. It is goodbye to a dream retirement. In short, death is goodbye to family and friends, dreams and hopes, ambitions and plans. How in the world, then, can death be gain?

What does Paul tell us? How does he tell us that death is gain? Look at verse 23, where he tells us that he has "the desire to depart [i.e., die] and be with Messiah." In other words, death is gain because it means the non-stop enjoyment of Christ Himself! What makes heaven heaven is God Himself! Teresa of Avila once said, "Wherever God is, there is heaven." As John Milton wrote, "Thy presence makes our paradise, and where Thou art is heaven." Samuel Rutherford explained it this way, "O my Lord Jesus Christ, if I could be in heaven without Thee, it would be a hell; and if I could be in hell, and have Thee still, it would be a heaven to me, for Thou art all the heaven I want." Finally, as Randy Alcorn put it, "To be with God—to know Him, to see Him—is the central, irreducible draw of heaven."

J.I. Packer once wrote that: "The essence of eternity as I conceive it—as it lies before me as my destination—is quite simply the joy of being with the Lord." In his book *Knowing God*, he gave what is probably the best definition of heaven ever penned:

What will make heaven to be heaven is the presence of Jesus, and of a reconciled divine Father who loves us for Jesus's sake no less than he loves Jesus himself. To see, and know, and love, and be loved by the Father and the Son, in company with the rest of God's vast family, is the whole essence of the Christian hope.

Christ is not a means to heaven; Christ is heaven. Therefore the Apostle Paul can say that death is gain because Christ was more precious to him than anything that life had to offer, or that death could take away. We see here, then, that saving faith must glorify God by treasuring Him more than health, wealth, and power. More than a good marriage, a good family, a good job. More than sex and entertainment, hopes and dreams, ambitions and plans. More than anything else imaginable.

To Live is Christ. Let us look at the first part of verse 21 —how does Paul say that Christ will be magnified in his life? We will explore this answer more in depth in a future chapter, but for now we will look at the answer he provides in the third chapter of Philippians:

> 7 But what things were to me gains, these I have counted, because of Messiah, loss. 8 Yes, indeed, and I count all things to be loss, because of the excellency of the knowledge of Messiah Jesus my Lord, because of whom I suffered the loss of all things, and do count them to be dung, that I may gain Messiah, 9 and be found in Him, not having my own righteousness, which is of the law, but that which is through faith in Christ—the righteousness that is from God by faith; 10 to know Him, and the

power of His resurrection, and the fellowship of His sufferings, being conformed to His death, 11 if anyhow I may attain to the resurrection of the dead.

(Phil. 3:7-11 NYLT)

There is much in this passage, but let's focus on the answer provided by verse 8: "Yet indeed I count all things to be loss, because of the excellency of the knowledge of Messiah Jesus my Lord, because of whom I suffered the loss of all things, and do count them to be dung, that I may gain Messiah." That is how saving faith glorifies God—by counting all things that this world has to offer as loss, as rubbish, as refuse, as dung, as trash compared to knowing and enjoying Christ Jesus the Lord.

And we see this illustrated in the very next chapter in Philippians:

> 11 Not that I say it in respect of want, for I did learn in things in which I am to be content. 12 I have known both to be humbled and I have known to abound. In everything and in all things I have learned the initiation secret both to be full and to be hungry, both to abound and to be in want. 13 For in all things I have strength in Christ's strengthening me.
>
> (Phil. 4:11-13 NYLT)

What is this secret of Christian contentment? That Christ is all we have. That He is more precious than all we could ever have. That He is more valuable than all we could ever lose. And therefore we can be content with nothing or with everything because Christ is our all in all. He is our life. This is why Paul can declare: "With Christ I have been crucified, and live no more do I, but Christ lives in me. And that which I now live in the flesh I live by faith in the Son of God, who agaped me and give Himself for me" (Gal. 2:20 NYLT). Not I, but Christ lives in me. This is how Christ is magnified in a believer's life.

Sorrowful, Yet Always Rejoicing:

Scripture is NOT the Prosperity Gospel. It does not preach that Christ is a genie who promises health, wealth, and power; who guarantees you your best life now. Rather, it is just the opposite. For in John 16:33, Jesus assures His elect that in this world they will have many tribulations (see also Matt. 10:24-25, 24:9; Jn. 15:18-21, 16:3), and in Acts 14:22 Paul tells us that it is only through such trials that we must enter the kingdom of God (see also 1 Pet. 4:12).

Do we, therefore, have a faith that will persevere to the finish line, come what may? Remember that the psalmist proclaims that, "In Your presence is fulness of joy, and at Your righthand are pleasures forevermore!" (Ps. 16:11). Not partial joy. Not temporary pleasures. But 100% joy now and forever! So how can we reconcile this precious reality of fulness of joy forever in God with the suffering and sorrow that we all face?

The secret of the Christian life—what sets it apart from any other religion or ethic—is what the Apostle Paul writes in 2 Corinthians 6:10—we are "sorrowful, yet always rejoicing." Joy in sorrow is not a contradiction. It is not the death knell of saving faith. Rather, it is the only thing that will sustain your faith when all your world falls away around you. I'm not talking about hope in future joy, though we have promise after promise guaranteeing that in Scripture. In Revelation, for instance, we are promised that "God will wipe away every tear from their eyes; there shall be no more death, nor sorrow, nor crying. There shall be no more pain, for the former things have passed away" (Rev. 21:4). Or in 2 Corinthians, chapter 4, beginning with verse 16 the Apostle Paul tells us:

> [16] Therefore, we faint not, but though our outward man decays, yet the inward is renewed day by day. [17] For the momentary lightness of our tribulation works for us a surpassing upon surpassing weight of glory age-enduring. [18] We are not looking to the things seen, but to the things not seen; for the things seen are temporary, but the things not seen are age-enduring.
> (2 Cor. 4:16-18 NYLT)

Those promises are beautiful and precious—no more pain, no more death, no more crying, a far more exceeding and eternal weight of glory! But they are not what this chapter is about. Rather, we are looking at how exactly a genuine, born-again believer can simultaneously have joy even in the midst of heart-wrenching loss and sorrow. Not comfort in promisees of future joy. But present-tense joy in the here and now in suffering, pain, and grief. Remember that Psalm 16:11 promises us that, "In Your presence is fulness of joy, and at Your righthand are pleasures forevermore!"

But is that even possible? Let us look at several examples from Scripture of this seemingly paradoxical faith—faith that rejoices in suffering.

The **first** is found in Job, chapter 1, which reads:

[13] And the day is that his sons and his daughters are eating and drinking wine in the house of their brother, the first-born. [14] And a messenger has come in unto Job and says, "The oxen have been plowing, and the donkeys feeding by their sides, [15] and Sheba falls upon them to take them, and the young men they have smitten by the mouth of the sword, and I am escaped—only I alone—to declare it to you."

[16] While this one is speaking, another also has come and says, "Fire of God has fallen from the heavens, and burns among the flock, and among the young men, and consumes them, and I am escaped—only I alone—to declare it to you."

[17] While this one is speaking, another also has come and says, "Chaldeans made three heads of companies to rush on the camels and take them, and the young men they have smitten by the mouth of the sword, and I am escaped—only I alone —to declare it to you."

[18] While this one is speaking another also has come and says, "Your sons and your daughters are eating and drinking wine in the house of their brother, the first-born. [19] And behold!—a great wind has come from over the wilderness and strikes against the four corners of the house, and it falls on the young, and they are dead. And I am escaped—only I alone—to declare it to you."

[20] And Job rises, tears his robe, shaves his head, and falls to the earth, and prostrates himself in worship. [21] And he says,

"Naked came I forth from the womb of my mother,
 And naked I turn back thither.
 Yahweh has given and Yahweh has taken:

Let the name of Yahweh be blessed."
²² In all this Job has not sinned, nor attributed folly to God.

(Job 1:13-22 NYLT)

Job lost everything except his wife and, up to this point, his health. And yet what did Job do? Verse 20 tells us that "he fell to the ground and worshipped." Verse 21 tells us that he blessed the name of Yahweh. How? And verse 22 tells us that he did not charge God with any wrongdoing for bringing these disasters upon him.

The **second** example comes from 2 Kings, chapter 4, where we find the story of Elisha the prophet praying that a barren woman would bear a son. She did so, but then we pick up the story in verse 18:

> ¹⁸ And the lad grows, and the day comes that he goes out unto his father, unto the reapers. ¹⁹ And he says to his father, "My head, my head" And he says to the young man, "Bear him unto his mother."
> ²⁰ And he bears him and brings him in unto his mother, and he sits on her knees till the noon and dies. ²¹ And she goes up and lays him on the bed of the man of God, and shuts the door upon him, and goes out ²² and calls to her husband and says, "Send, I pray you, to me one of the young men and one of the donkeys, and I run unto the man of God and return."
> ²³ And he says, "Why are you going unto him today? It is neither the new moon nor sabbath?" And she says, "Shalom!" ²⁴ And she saddles the donkey and says unto her young man, "Lead, and

go, do not restrain your riding for me, except I have said so to you."

²⁵ And she goes and comes in unto the man of God, unto Mount Carmel, and it comes to pass, at the man of God seeing her afar off, that he says to Gehazi his young man, "Behold!—this Shunammite! ²⁶ Now, run, I pray you, to meet her and say to her, "Is there shalom with you? Is there shalom with your husband? Is there shalom with the child?" And she says, "Shalom!"

²⁷ And she comes in unto the man of God on the hill, and lays hold of his feet, and Gehazi comes near to thrust her away. But the man of God says, "Let her alone, for her soul is bitter to her, and Yahweh has hidden it from me, and has not declared it to me."

(2 Kings 4:18-27 NYLT)

So you have the Shunammite woman's faith to be simultaneously "bitter" (vs. 27) while also experiencing "shalom" (vs. 26)? The Hebrew word *shalom* means, literally, *peace*, though the NIV84 translates it as "'everything is all right'" and the NKJV as "'it is well.'"

Henrietta, the wife of R.C. Ryle (who was the Bishop of Liverpool 130 years ago), had verse 26—"It is well"—written on her tombstone. How? This is also the verse that Horatio Stafford based his hymn *It Is Well With My Soul*! after his four daughters drowned at sea. How?

The **third** example is found in Luke, chapter 6, where we find the Beatitudes of Jesus' Sermon on the Plain:

²² "Blessed are you when men shall hate you,
And when they shall separate you for exclusion,

And shall reproach you,
And shall cast forth your name as evil,
For the Son of Man's sake.
23 Rejoice in that day and leap!
For behold!—your wage is great in the heaven,
For according to these things their fathers were doing to the prophets.

(Lk. 6:22-23 NYLT)

Unlike the seed that fell on stony ground, when trials and tribulations come our way we are to rejoice and leap for joy! And not in a future day, but in the very day that those trials and tribulations come—"rejoice *in that day*"! James, the half-brother of Jesus, tells us to, "count it all joy when you fall into various trials!" (Jas. 1:2) Peter tells us to rejoice the fiery trials which come our way (1 Pet. 4:12-13). How is this possible?

But we see that the early church did, in fact, know how to do this. For instance, when the Twelve Apostles were imprisoned and beaten by the Jewish religious authorities for preaching in the name of Jesus, "they departed from the presence of the council, rejoicing that they were counted worthy to suffer shame for [Jesus] name" (Acts 6:41). Acts 16 tells us that Paul and Silas were severely beaten with rods (vs. 22-23) and then thrown into the deepest, darkest cell with their feet fastened in the stocks (vs. 24). And yet, verse 25 tells us that even as late as midnight Paul and Silas were praying and singing hymns to God! How?

The **fourth** example comes from 2 Corinthians, chapter 8, where the Apostle Paul is describing to the Corinthian church the generosity of the church at Philippi to the poor and needy of the Jerusalem church. Beginning with verse 1 we read:

> ¹ And we make known to you, brethren, the grace of God that has been given in the assemblies of Macedonia, ² because in much trial of tribulation the abundance of their joy and their deep poverty did abound to the riches of their generosity. ³ Because I testify that, according to their power, and above their power, they were willing of themselves, ⁴ begging us with much entreaty to receive the grace and the fellowship of the deaconing to the saints.
>
> (2 Cor. 8:1-4 NYLT)

Despite "much trial of tribulation" and "deep poverty" (vs. 2), Paul tells us that their joy abounded all the more, resulting in the "riches of their generosity" (vs. 2) in which they freely gave above their means (vs. 3). How?

The **fifth** and final example comes from the Apostle Paul himself. In 1 Corinthians 4 where Paul gives a brief autobiographical sketch of his trials and tribulations as a missionary church planter:

> ⁹ For I think that God did set forth us, the apostles, last—as appointed to death, because we became a theater exhibition to the world, both angelic messengers and men. ¹⁰ We are fools because of Christ, but you wise in Christ! We are without strength, but you are strong! You are glorious, but we are dishonored! ¹¹ Unto the present hour we both hunger and thirst, and are naked, and are struck with fists, and wander about homeless.

¹² And we labor, working with our own hands. Being reviled, we bless; being persecuted, we forbear; ¹³ being spoken evil of, we entreat; as filth of the world we did become as filth of the world, the scum of all things until now.

(1 Cor. 4:9-13 NYLT)

2 Corinthians, chapter 11, provides us in even fuller glimpse into his sufferings and persecutions:

²³ Are they deacons of Messiah?—as beside myself I speak—I more; in labors more abundantly, in stripes above measure, in prisons more frequently, in deaths many times. ²⁴ From Jews five times I received forty stripes minus one. ²⁵ Three times was I beaten with rods; once was I stoned; three times I was shipwrecked; a night and a day I have passed in the deep; ²⁶ in journeys many times, in perils of rivers, in perils of robbers, in perils from kindred, in perils from ethnic groups, in perils in the city, in perils in the wilderness, in perils in the sea, in perils among false brethren; ²⁷ in labor and painful toil, in sleeplessness many times, in hunger and thirst, in fastings many times, in cold and nakedness; ²⁸ apart from the things external, the pressure upon me daily is the care of all the assemblies. ²⁹ Who is infirm, and I am not infirm? Who is stumbled, and I am not on fire?

(2 Cor. 11:23-29 NYLT)

Finally, in Romans, the Apostle Paul tells us that he has "great sorrow and continual grief in my heart" for his Jewish brethren who are not saved (Rom. 9:2). This isn't just "great sorrow and...grief" only during times of imprisonment, beatings, and hardships. No, Paul specifically states that this is "continual" sorrow and grief. And yet, in Philippians this same Paul tells us, "Rejoice in the Lord always! Again, I will say, rejoice!" (Phil. 4:4). How?

The Joy of Yahweh is Our Stronghold:

In the book that bears his name, we find Nehemiah telling the weeping Israelites, "...be not grieved, for the joy of Yahweh is your stronghold!" (Neh. 8:10 NYLT). We will look at just three ways in which the joy in Yahweh is our stronghold in suffering.

First, the joy in Yahweh is our stronghold in suffering because our sufferings are Christ sufferings. This sounds almost blasphemous. Almost too good to be true. But Paul tells believers that they "suffer with Him [Christ], that we may also be glorified together *with Him*" (Rom. 8:17). In another place he tells us that "the sufferings of Christ abound in us" (2 Cor. 1:5). Still elsewhere he tells us that he considers his life of self-righteousness and self-merit to be rubbish so "that I might know Him [Christ]...and the fellowship of His sufferings" (Phil. 3:10). Finally, Peter tells us to "[13] rejoice to the extent that you participate of Christ's sufferings...[14]...blessed are you, for the Spirit of glory and of God rests upon you" (1 Pet. 4:13-14).

Our sufferings are, in fact, Christ's sufferings:

- We suffer with Christ (Rom. 8:17).
- Christ's sufferings abound in us (2 Cor. 1:5).
- We have fellowship in His sufferings (Phi. 3:10).
- We participate in Christ's sufferings (1 Pet. 4:13).

Now Scripture provides two grounds for these audacious statements. The first is that when we are persecuted for being believers, our persecutors are really persecuting Christ. We see this most clearly when the risen Christ appeared to the Apostle Paul on the Damascus road. Up until this moment Paul was not a believer but was instead a fire-breathing persecutor of believers on his way to Damascus to kill and imprison Christians. But Jesus appeared to him and said, "'Saul, Saul, why are you persecuting Me?'" (Acts 26:14). Not, "Why are you persecuting the Church?" Not, "Why are you persecuting Christians?" But, "Why are you persecuting Me?" So Christ Himself is suffering persecution along with us when we are persecuted for the sake of His name.

But the second reason why our sufferings are, in fact, Christ's sufferings is our union with Christ. Galatians 2:20 tells us that though we live, yet it is not us who live but Christ in us. Similarly, Colossians 3:3-4 tells us that our life is hidden with Christ in God and, therefore, He is now our life. Ephesians 5:30-32 tells us that, as Christ's Bride, we are members of His body—flesh of His flesh and bone of His bones—for the two shall become one flesh.

Therefore, whether our sufferings are the result of religious persecution or the result of living in a fallen world —Christ suffers with us. Our sufferings are His sufferings. He is not participating in our sufferings, but rather we are participating in His. When we wept, He has already wept first. When we experience pain, He already experienced it first. When our hearts are breaking, His heart already broke with grief. For Isaiah 53:4 tells us that Christ bore our grief and carried our sorrows.

But through the storm of our grief and pain upon Calvary, Christ emerged victorious and is therefore able to comfort us. 2 Corinthians, chapter 1, reads:

> ³ Blessed is God—the Father of our Lord Jesus Messiah and the Father of mercies and God of all comfort—⁴ who is comforting us in all our tribulation, for our being able to comfort those in any tribulation through the comfort with which we are comforted ourselves by God. ⁵ Because, as the sufferings of the Messiah abound to us, so through the Messiah also abounds our comfort.
>
> (2 Cor. 1:3-5 NYLT)

Therefore, just as our sufferings are Christ's sufferings, so His comfort is now also our comfort! He draws close to us, surrounds us with His loving arms, and gives us the peace of His presence. John Patton was a missionary in the 1800s to the cannibals of the New Hebrides. After years of largely futile ministry on one of the islands, the majority of the Natives sought his life. A few of them, however, told him to climb a tree while they distracted and mislead those who hunted his life. The following is his account of that night in his autobiography:

> Being entirely at the mercy of such doubtful and vacillating friends, I, though perplexed, felt it best to obey. I climbed into the tree and was left there alone in the bush. The hours I spent there live all before me as if it were but of yesterday. I heard the frequent discharging of muskets, and the yells of the Savages. Yet I sat there among the branches, as safe as in the arms of Jesus. Never, in all my sorrows, did my Lord draw nearer to me, and speak more soothingly in my soul, than when the moonlight flickered among those chestnut leaves, and the night air played on my throbbing brow, as I

told all my heart to Jesus. Alone, yet not alone! If it be to glorify my God, I will not grudge to spend many nights alone in such a tree, to feel again my Savior's spiritual presence, to enjoy His consoling fellowship. If thus thrown back upon your own soul, alone, all alone, in the midnight, in the bush, in the very embrace of death itself, have you a Friend that will not fail you then? (p. 200)

Intimate fellowship in the comforting presence of our Savior and Friend is the first reason why joy in Yahweh is our stronghold in suffering.

Secondly, the joy of Yahweh is our stronghold in suffering because it prunes us, it purifies us, it strips us, of all but Christ. Underlying this second point—and, indeed, underlying any joy the believer has in the midst of suffering, is God's absolute sovereignty. For if our suffering were merely the result of the randomness of nature or the happenstance of men's evil desires, then they would quickly unravel into purposelessness, and therefore meaninglessness, and therefore despairing madness. Only in the hands of a Master Craftsmen can we have any hope of purpose and, therefore, any hope of joy.

And the Bible is emphatically clear that God is the absolute sovereign author of everything that was, is, and is to come; what He wills, He does: "'for I am God, and there is no other; I am God, and there is none like Me, declaring the end from the beginning and from ancient times things not yet done, saying, "My counsel shall stand, and I will accomplish all My purpose"'" (Is. 46:9-10). He watches over His word to perform it (Jer. 1:12), and no purpose of His can be thwarted (Job 42:4; Ecc. 7:13). "All the inhabitants of the earth are reputed as nothing; He does according to His will in the army of heaven and among the inhabitants of the earth. No one can restrain His hand or say to Him, 'What have You done?'" (Dan. 4:35). "All that Yahweh pleased He has done—in the heavens and in earth, in the seas and all deep places" (Ps. 135:6 NYLT) as He "works all things according to the counsel of His will" (Eph. 1:11).

God is therefore the absolutely sovereign author of every detail pertaining to all things, including but not limited to wind (Lk. 8:25), lightning (Job 36:32), earthquakes (Acts 16:26; Rev. 16:18), snow (Ps. 147:16), frogs (Ex. 8:1-15), gnats (Ex. 8:16-19), flies (Ex. 8:20-32), locusts (Ex. 10:1-12), quail (Ex. 16:6-8), worms (Jonah 4:7), fish (Jonah 2:10), sparrows (Matt. 10:29), grass (Ps. 147:8), plants (Jonah 4:6), famine (Ps. 105:16), the sun (Josh. 10:12-13), prison doors (Acts 5:19), blindness (Ex. 4:11; Lk. 18:42), deafness (Ex. 4:11; Mk. 7:37), paralysis (Lk. 5:24-25), fever (Matt. 8:15), the sickness of children (2 Sam. 12:15), every disease (Matt. 4:23), travel plans (Jas. 4:13-15), the rolling of dice (Prov. 16:33), the loss or gain of money (1 Sam. 2:7), the hearts of kings (Prov. 21:1; Dan. 2:21), nations (Ps. 33:10), murderers (Acts 4:27-28), spiritual deadness (Eph. 2:4-5), the slaughter of His people (Ps. 44:11), the suffering of His saints (1 Pet. 4:19), the persecution of His children (Heb. 12:4-7), the repentance of souls (2 Tim. 2:25), the gift of faith (Phil. 1:29), the pursuit of holiness (Phil. 3:12-13), the maturity of the elect (Heb. 6:3), the giving of life and taking in death (1 Sam. 2:6), and the crucifixion of His Son (Acts 4:27-28).

Consequently, the suffering and sorrow of God's elect do not rest upon chance nor upon the will of men, but solely upon God's sovereign authorship—for He has appointed who shall suffer (Rev. 6:11), when they shall suffer (Jn.

7:30; Acts 18:9-10), where they shall suffer (Lk. 9:30, 13:33), and what kind of sufferings they shall experience (Mk. 9:13; Jn. 21:19; Acts 9:16, 13:29)—who among them shall die of hunger, with the sword, be lead into captivity, and be eaten up by beasts (Jer. 15:2-3). The saints of God, therefore, are immortal until their work is done (Ps. 139:16; Heb. 9:27; Jas. 4:13-16).

As a result, suffering for the believer is a gift from God. That is what Paul told the church at Philippi: "For to you it has been granted on behalf of Christ, not only to believe in Him, but also to suffer for His sake" (Phil. 1:29). Peter boldly declares that we "suffer according to the will of God" (1 Pet. 4:19; see also 3:17). Elsewhere Peter tells us that we are called by God to suffer (1 Pet. 2:21; 3:9). Therefore, all suffering and sorrow, pain and grief is a gift from God. A calling by God. Willed by God. Why? There are more reasons to our suffering than we can presently imagine, and we will never fully know the reasons why this side of heaven.

But Scripture is clear that—with the very same love with which He loves His Son—God the Father orchestrates all of our suffering in order to prune us, refine us, and strip us of all but Christ. Yes, it is to make us holy (Rom. 5:1-5; Heb. 12:3-11; 2 Pet. 1:5-9). But holiness is never the end in and of itself. Rather, it is so that we might find full and lasting satisfaction in Christ as our treasure. People often say that God will never give them more than they can bear; that God entrusts them with their suffering because He knows that they can handle it. That's blasphemous.

Rather, the Christian responds as the Apostle Paul does in 2 Corinthians 12:

> [7] And that I might not be exalted overmuch by the exceeding greatness of the revelations, there was

given to me a thorn in the flesh, a messenger of the Adversary, that he might buffet me, that I might not be exalted overmuch. 8 Concerning this thing I did call upon the Lord three times that it might depart from me. 9 And He said to me, "My grace is sufficient for you, for My power is perfected in infirmity." Most gladly, therefore, will I rather boast in my infirmities, that the power of the Messiah may rest on me. 10 Wherefore I am well pleased in infirmities, in mistreatments, in necessities, in persecutions, in distresses—for Christ; for whenever I am infirm, then I am powerful.

(2 Cor. 12:7-10 NYLT)

God's strength is made perfect in our weakness. In our sufferings. In our pain. God is most glorified when, truly, all we have is Christ. When He is our desire. Our delight. Our joy. Our treasure. Though we may have "the sentence of death in ourselves," it is so "that we should not trust in ourselves but in God" (2 Cor. 1:9). Therefore most gladly will we boast in our pain and suffering, sorrows and grief, for when we are nothing, then Christ is magnified. When Christ is more precious to us than anything life has to offer or that death can take away, then He is most glorified.

This is the secret of the Christian life—contentment in Christ. We see this illustrated in Philippians, chapter 4, beginning with verse 11:

11 Not that I say it in respect of want, for I did learn in things in which I am to be content. 12 I have known both to be humbled and I have known to abound. In everything and in all things I have learned the initiation secret both to be full and to

be hungry, both to abound and to be in want.
13 For in all things I have strength in Christ's strengthening me.

(Phil. 4:11-13 NYLT)

The key, therefore, to being "sorrowful, yet always rejoicing" (2 Cor. 6:10) is that Christ is all we have. That He is more precious than anything life has to offer or that death can take away. He is our life, our contentment. The point of suffering is to drive us to Christ, to know Him intimately (Job 42:5), and therefore the more we treasure Him in our suffering, the more joy we have in our suffering. Only joy in Christ can make suffering pleasurable.

Third and finally, the joy in Yahweh is our stronghold in suffering because we magnify Christ's worth to the world. This builds on the point just made. Suffering not only internally strips us of everything but Christ, but then in living out that reality in the midst of suffering is a vibrant, living testimony to the beauty of Christ to others:

> I now rejoice in my sufferings for you, and fill up in my flesh the things lacking of the tribulations of the Messiah for His body, which is the assembly.
> (Col. 1:24 NYLT)

What does Paul mean here when he says he "fill[s] up in my flesh the things lacking of the tribulations of the Messiah"? We know he isn't saying that Christ's atonement on the Cross was somehow deficient, for Christ Himself said that "'It is finished'" (Jn. 19:30) upon Calvary's hill. Therefore we know Paul isn't saying that he is somehow suffering to save people from sin and death, for the author of Hebrews tells us that "Christ was offered once to bear the sins of many" (Heb. 9:28). There is only one final and completed sacrifice for sins—Jesus Christ upon the cross.

So we know what Paul doesn't mean, but the question still remains as to what he does mean. Paul uses nearly identical language in Philippians 2:30 in commending Epaphroditus to the church at Philippi for his sacrifices in ministering to Paul in prison in Rome: "because for the work of Christ he came close to death, not regarding his life, to supply what was lacking in your service to me." What was lacking in the ministry of the Philippian church to Paul? Nothing but a visible manifestation of that service. In other words, they couldn't all go to Rome to serve Paul, so they sent Epaphroditus to Paul as their representative to show Paul how much they love and care for him.

That is precisely what Paul is saying in Colossians 1:24. Not that Christ's sufferings and death were insufficient, but rather that Paul, in his own sufferings and pending martyrdom, is visibly demonstrating to those who never witnessed the horror of Calvary what the glory and worth of the love of God is. A pain-free life doesn't show anybody the love of Christ. Joyless sorrow in the midst of heartache doesn't show anybody the love of Christ. Rather, what the world needs most is the infinite value of the love of God by how Christians are "sorrowful, yet always rejoicing" (2 Cor. 6:10). It is only when we show that Christ is our treasure in good times and bad, in carefree days and when the floor gives way beneath us, when we have everything and when we have nothing, that they will want what—or, more accurately, Who—we have.

Concluding Implications:

I conclude with a portion of the funeral sermon given by George Muller, a famous pastor in the 1800s, upon his wife's death:

> The last portion of scripture which I read to my precious wife was this: "The Lord God is a sun and shield, the Lord will give grace and glory, no good thing will he withhold from them that walk uprightly." Now, if we have believed in the Lord Jesus Christ, we have received grace, we are partakers of grace, and to all such he will give glory also. I said to myself, with regard to the latter part, "no good thing will he withhold from them that walk uprightly"—I am in myself a poor worthless sinner, but I have been saved by the blood of Christ; and I do not live in sin, I walk uprightly before God. Therefore, if it is really good for me, my darling wife will be raised up again; sick as she is. God will restore her again. But if she is not restored again, then it would not be a good thing for me [to have her]. And so my heart was at rest. I was satisfied with God. And all this springs, as I have often said before, from taking God at his word, believing what he says.

Look at what he said—he is satisfied in God because he knows that God will only do what is good, what is best, for him because he is clothed with Christ's righteousness.

Or, to put it another way, all of our grief and sorrow, pain and suffering, are blood-bought gifts purchased by Christ on Calvary for they are blessings and privileges designed by God for our good and joy. Therefore, if God sacrificed His one and only Son to obtain them, then they must be necessary for my joy in treasuring Him supremely.

Or, to put it another way, the only troubles that God permits in the lives of His children are those that will bring more pleasure than trouble with them—when all things are considered.

Or, to put it in yet a final way, if we suffer it is because God values something in us greater than our physical comfort and health that He in His infinite wisdom and kindness knows can only be attained by means of our physical affliction and the lessons of submission and dependency and trust in Him that we learn from it.

Therefore, with George Muller who found much comfort in this hymn, let us sing:

> Best of blessings He'll provide us
> Nought but good shall e'er betide us,
> Safe to glory He will guide us,
> Oh how He loves!

Let us kiss Christ—the Rose of Sharon—even in the midst of the thorns as we sing:

> [1] In Jesus I found such a wonderful friend,
> He satisfies all of my need;
> He's more than my heart ever could comprehend,
> O He is a Savior indeed.

Chorus:
> He is the rose of Sharon,
> Fragrant and sweet to me,
> He is my light when shadows fall,
> Savior and keeper is He;
> He is the rose of Sharon,
> He is my all in all.

Are My Babies in Heaven?

2 My constant Companion, my Counselor too,
My High Priest most holy is He;
The King of my soul and my Advocate true,
My Savior forever will be. [Chorus]

3 Far more than the trifles that earth can afford,
In Christ my Redeemer I see;
In Him all the treasures of Heaven are stored,
Eternal His praises shall be. [Chorus]

Nathan W. Tucker

ON CHRIST THE SOLID ROCK I STAND
By Edward Mote

1 My hope is built on nothing less
Than Jesus Christ, my righteousness;
I dare not trust the sweetest frame,
But wholly lean on Jesus' name.

Chorus: On Christ, the solid Rock, I stand;
All other ground is sinking sand,
All other ground is sinking sand.

2 When darkness veils His lovely face,
I rest on His unchanging grace;
In every high and stormy gale,
My anchor holds within the veil.

3 His oath, His covenant, His blood,
Support me in the whelming flood;
When all around my soul gives way,
He then is all my hope and stay.

4 When He shall come with trumpet sound,
Oh, may I then in Him be found;
In Him, my righteousness, alone,
Faultless to stand before the throne.

COMING 2026!

CATECHIZING AS DOXOLOGY:
THE CHRISTIAN FAITH IN FULL BLOOM

A 365 QUESTION CATECHISM AS A DAILY FAMILY DEVOTIONAL BASED ON THE 1689 2ND LONDON BAPTIST CONFESSION OF FAITH

OTHER BOOKS BY NATHAN TUCKER:

You Must Be Born Again! An Evangelistic Exposition of John 3:1-8

Agape: The Essence of Saving Faith

The Five Solas: An Expository Exhortation

Julia's Christmas Carol

Letters From Cell No. 73

Constitutional Musings: An Anthology of Legal Columns

We the People: The Only Cure to Judicial Activism

www.ingramcontent.com/pod-product-compliance
Lightning Source LLC
Chambersburg PA
CBHW070550050426
42450CB00011B/2797